Jackie Jones has worked at Edinburgh University Press for many years. In addition to her publishing career, she has undertaken numerous vegan cookery, restaurant-level courses and masterclasses in the UK, and has a Vegan Diploma and Advanced Vegan Diploma from Demuths Cookery School, Bath.

SCOTTISH Vegan Baking

JACKIE JONES

BIRLINN

CONTENTS

INTRODUCTION

Welcome to *Scottish Vegan Baking*! So many people enjoy baking – whether it's bread for sandwiches and morning toast, biscuits for a cuppa with friends, or scones and cakes for a family Sunday afternoon tea at home – and there are now many books available on vegan baking to give the baker confidence when moving from dairy-based recipes. But this is the first to focus on all the classic Scottish bakes, made vegan. In this book, the sequel to *The Scottish Vegan Cookbook*, I have taken some of the nation's favourites, often named for the region from which they hale – from Abernethy biscuits to Selkirk bannock, Border tart to Tantallon cakes, Ecclefechan tarts to Dundee cake – and given them the special vegan makeover.

Whether you are going, or have gone, vegan for the animals, for the environment or for your health – or all three – have dairy-free needs, or are baking for vegan friends, family, a bake sale or work colleagues, vegan baking is done differently. The ingredients are, of course, different – there's no dairy butter, dairy milk, dairy cream, eggs, honey or gelatine – but the baking methods, which I take you through in each recipe, are also different.

To get you started, I show you which substitutes you need for dairy ingredients and how to use them, which is followed by a 'How To' section with baking tips to help ensure your breads and cakes rise and your baking reaches delicious perfection! The recipes are then gathered into different sections, starting with a range of basics including pastry, whipped cream, caramel and cake toppings that you can use time and time again. There are recipes for breads and biscuits to make including baps and a fermented barm loaf using Scottish ale! And classic Scottish cakes such as marmalade cake and sticky gingerbread as well as vegan versions of the all-time greats – carrot cake and Victoria sponge – and a celebration chocolate cake.

I have included vegan adaptations of several different versions of scones and shortbread to showcase the historical and regional range, and one of my favourite shortbread recipes in the book is also gluten-free. There are a few twists, including cranachan (that gorgeous blend of raspberries, whisky, cream and oatmeal) both in a tart and a cheesecake, as well as classics like empire biscuits and digestives. For those looking for healthier options there are flapjacks which are low in refined sugar, on-the-go oat bars for a post-workout pick-me-up or lunch boxes, and divine beetroot and chocolate truffles. My favourite feature of the book is the section on holding your own 'cookie shine' which is a traditional Scottish afternoon tea made vegan, with a tempting array of delicate filled sandwiches, little bite-sized cakes and moreish treats.

Throughout *Scottish Vegan Baking* I have added in some nutritional guidance about the healthy properties of different baking ingredients such as fruits, nuts, seeds, spices and – yes! – the occasional vegetable, such as naturally sweet beetroot and carrots. I hope there is something here for everyone, whether you are new to vegan baking, have an interest in Scottish culinary heritage, or are a seasoned vegan baker looking for new inspiration.

For the animals, with my hopes and wishes,

Jackie

VEGAN BAKING INGREDIENTS

Most traditional sweet baking involves fat of some kind – often dairy butter – sugar, flour and eggs in varying proportions. When it comes to vegan baking, we not only have to substitute the dairy elements which have different properties in the bake, we generally have to change some preparation techniques as well, although some methods, such as mixing, 'creaming' or 'rubbing in' are also used when veganising a bake. And each ingredient has a special role to play. Vegan soft butter is used in shortbread, for example, whereas a vegan hard 'block' butter is needed for making pastry, and oil or melted vegan butter is used in making cakes.

In Scottish baking, especially for bread and gingerbread, beer or ale can be used as a raising agent and bring moisture to a loaf instead of using water. Scottish baking makes great use of Scotland's staple: oats – in oatcakes, bread, crumbles and flapjacks – as well as whisky for a fiery kick. Other flavour hits come from ground ginger, cinnamon and mixed spice. My recipes also use fresh fruit – including apples and pears, raspberries and strawberries, oranges and lemons – as well as the occasional beetroot! Dried fruits have been used in baking recipes for hundreds of years in cakes, sweet loaves, tarts and tray bakes. Nuts – especially walnuts, hazelnuts and almonds – feature in the recipes that follow as do seeds which have many beneficial properties.

Below are ingredients you may use in these bakes, including some of the substitutes that are commonly used in vegan baking.

BUTTERS & OILS

Substitutes for dairy butter include:

almond butter
coconut butter
cold-pressed rapeseed oil
extra-virgin olive oil
margarine
peanut butter
sunflower oil
tahini
vegan 'butter'

Vegan butters and margarines are usually a blend of oils such as sunflower, coconut, rapeseed and olive oil. Try to avoid using too much tropical oil such as coconut oil and palm oil, which are high in saturated fat, and if using margarines containing palm oil check whether or not they are from certified renewable sources.

My go-to vegan butters are Naturli when a block butter is called for (although Stork can also be used) and Vitalite when a soft vegan butter is called for. I tend to use sunflower oil or olive oil for cakes and coconut butter (not to be confused with coconut oil) in a cheesecake for its setting properties.

EGG SUBSTITUTES

Egg yolks have emulsifying/binding properties and egg whites have raising properties; eggs also add moisture. In substituting eggs, we can use a number of different alternatives:

Binding

One egg can generally be substituted by 4 tablespoons of a vegan alternative (or 60g) for binding ingredients together. These include:

Apple purée
Banana (½ banana per replacement egg)
Buttermilk (1 teaspoon of lemon juice or apple cider vinegar added to the stated amount of soya or other plant-based milk and set aside to curdle)
Chia seed egg – 1 tablespoon of chia seeds mixed with 3 tablespoons of cold water and left for 5 minutes to gel
Flax seed egg – 1 tablespoon of flax seeds mixed with 3 tablespoons of cold water and left for 5 minutes to gel
Silken tofu
Yoghurt (plain, unsweetened soya yoghurt or other plant-based yoghurt)

RAISING AGENTS

Raising agents have aerating properties to give lift to bakes such as cakes and muffins. There are various ways to replace the raising agent provided by eggs including:

Ale/beer/stout
Aquafaba – the liquid from a can of cooked beans, especially chickpeas
Baking powder + an acid such as lemon juice or apple cider vinegar
Bicarbonate of soda + an acid such as lemon juice or apple cider vinegar
Sparkling water

In the recipes that follow I mostly use baking powder together with an acid which reacts with the baking powder to create a rise in cakes and bakes. I find the results more consistent and stable than aquafaba, for example.

FLOUR

While white flour is used in many of the recipes, there are some alternatives which retain some beneficial nutrients mostly taken out in milling white flour. I tend to opt for wholemeal varieties where possible which, as the name implies, contain the entirety of the wheat including the bran. I use white flour where it produces a better bake, texture or appearance, such as in certain breads or in my Victoria Sponge. White flour include strong white bread flour, plain white flours and white self-raising flour. Some recipes also include ground almonds, rice flour and rye flour.

MILK

My go-to substitute for dairy milk in baking is soya milk, used both to loosen a mixture and to add moisture. Soya milk has good binding properties and contains more protein than other plant milks, although you can also use oat milk or almond milk.

SWEETENERS

There are a range of natural fruit sugars and unrefined or minimally refined sugars that you can use in vegan baking in addition to refined sugar. These include:

Dried fruit: apple rings, apricots, cherries, coconut, dates, figs, peaches, prunes, raisins and sultanas
Fresh fruit: apples, bananas, blackberries, blackcurrants, blueberries, pears, strawberries
Sugar: black treacle, blackstrap molasses, caster sugar, dark muscovado sugar, date sugar, date syrup, demerara sugar, elderflower syrup, maple syrup, soft brown sugar
Vegetables: carrots, beetroot

THICKENERS

The main thickening agents that are used in these recipes are cornflour and flax seed egg. You can also use chia seeds, which expand when mixed with water to form a gel.

OTHER BAKING INGREDIENTS

Chocolate: cacao powder (unroasted cocoa powder) or organic cocoa powder (such as Green & Black's), vegan dark chocolate (70%) (such as Green & Black's)
Cream: soya cream, oat cream
Natural flavourings: pure almond extract, pure vanilla extract, rose water
Nuts: almonds, brazil nuts, cashew nuts, hazelnuts, pecans, pistachios, walnuts
Seeds: poppy seeds, pumpkin seeds, sesame seeds, sunflower seeds
Spices: caraway seeds, ground cardamom, ground cinnamon, fennel seeds, ground ginger, ground mixed spice, ground nutmeg

NUTRITION

While most cakes and bakes are sweet treats, the recipes include some ingredients which contain good nutrition.

Protein: nuts and nut butters, seeds and seed butters, soya milk and soya cream, oat milk and oat cream, tofu and wholemeal flour
Iron: beetroot, currants, dried apricots, dried figs, flax seeds, nuts, prunes, raisins, raw cacao powder, seeds
Calcium: almonds, brazil nuts, cinnamon, dates, lemon zest, prunes, sesame seeds

HOW TO USE THIS BOOK

Baking – vegan baking included – generally requires precision. Weigh and measure according to the recipes using accurate – preferably digital – scales and make sure you don't leave ingredients out. All ingredients are readily available from local shops, health food shops or supermarkets except, perhaps, candied lemon peel which can be bought online (recipe alternative also given).

It is best to read the recipe all the way through and gather all the ingredients together before you start; you can weigh each ingredient into separate bowls if you like.

Many of the recipes call for the ingredients to be brought together with your hands (e.g. 'to form a dough'). These need to be clean hands!

All spoon measurements are level unless otherwise stated (e.g. 'heaped').

Use ingredients at room temperature unless otherwise stated (e.g. 'fridge-cold'; 'chilled').

Sift flour to ensure no lumps appear in the batter and break up any sugar clumps with a fork when mixing cake batters.

Try to use unwaxed oranges and lemons where a recipe calls for zest.

With cakes, muffins and cupcakes, try not to overmix the batter to ensure a good rise. Once you have filled your baking tin or muffin cases, tap the baking tin on a hard surface on the bottom to distribute the batter evenly before baking.

Recipes that include bicarbonate of soda and lemon juice or apple cider vinegar in the batter need to go into the oven as quickly as possible to create the rise.

When lining your baking tin with greaseproof baking paper, scrunch up the baking paper first and then press it into the tin.

The symbol {Prepare in advance} has been added to some recipes to indicate that you need to – or can – make something ahead of the day you want to serve it.

Oven temperatures are given for standard ovens in Celsius. While you will know how your own oven behaves, generally for fan ovens you need to reduce the temperature by around 20 degrees, e.g. 180°C would be 160°C for a fan oven. I recommend buying a thermometer (such as ChefAid) that you can put in your oven if you have a fickle fan oven.

Bake cakes, tarts, scones, bread, etc. on the middle shelf of your oven unless the recipe indicates otherwise.

Cover cakes or fruit loaves with kitchen foil if they are catching on the top while in the oven, especially if dried fruit is in the mixture.

For cakes, set a timer for the shortest period of cooking time and test with a skewer (most recipes require a cake tester or skewer to come out clean or with a few crumbs); add no more than 5 further minutes at a time to the cooking time if the cake is not yet cooked and keep testing until fully baked. Be careful not to open the oven during the minimum recommended baking time, especially for cakes, and generally keep the oven open for the shortest possible time if you are testing a bake with a skewer so the oven doesn't drop in temperature.

If your cake – especially a sponge cake – 'domes' in the middle while baking, as opposed to just having a slight curve, and/or 'splits' across the top, this is likely to be because the baking tin has heated up too quickly and is cooking the cake mixture faster at the edges. Insulate the outside of your baking tin with a thick layer of kitchen foil or what's known as a baking 'belt' or collar before baking the cake to compensate.

0

BASICS

ALMOND CREAM

{Prepare in advance}

Makes around 325ml

Prep time: 10 minutes + overnight soaking

This is a versatile nut-based thick pouring cream (like double cream) for spooning over sweet tarts and flans as well as puddings, crumbles and fresh fruit salad.

INGREDIENTS

100g blanched almonds

250ml soya milk

2 teaspoons vanilla extract

2 tablespoons maple syrup

METHOD

Place the almonds in a bowl, cover them with cold water and soak overnight in the fridge.

Once soaked, drain and rinse the almonds then add them to a blender jug with the soya milk, vanilla extract and maple syrup. Blend on high until smooth. Pour into a bowl, cover, and refrigerate until needed. The cream will keep in the fridge for 2–3 days.

If you want a runnier cream, add a little more milk at the blending stage.

A word about . . . almonds

Almonds are rich in nutrients including magnesium, vitamin E, copper and manganese as well as good (unsaturated) fats. Most of the nutrients are contained within the skin. This recipe calls for blanched almonds; but go for almonds with their skins on where possible – e.g. for snacking, adding to muesli, in other cakes and bakes.

APPLE SAUCE

Makes around 850g

Prep time: 25 minutes

Cooking time: 10–15 minutes

It is useful to have apple sauce on hand as a substitute for the binding function of egg yolk. Puréed apples help add moisture. See the recipe for Pear and Ginger Cake (p. 110). You can also use apple sauce as a topping on pancakes or ice cream, on muesli or porridge, or just on its own with vegan custard or cream.

INGREDIENTS

8 medium cooking apples (about 1.25kg)

A good squeeze of lemon juice

8 tablespoons hot water + extra if needed

5 tablespoons maple syrup + extra if needed

METHOD

Place the apples in a large pan and cover with cold water. Add the lemon juice (this helps to stop the apples from browning). Peel, core, quarter and roughly chop the apples one at a time, placing them back in the water. Depending on the type, size and quality of the apples, you will have about 850g in total.

Once you have prepared all of the apples, drain the cold water away. Add 6 tablespoons of the hot water and the maple syrup and bring to a medium-high heat. Once the apples start to cook, reduce the heat to low and stir regularly to allow the apples to break down. Cook until softened, about 10–15 minutes, adding the 2 further tablespoons of water, and a little more if needed, to produce a soft apple pulp. Taste and add further sweetener if you like. If you are using windfall apples, they can be quite tart.

Remove from the heat and press the apples through a sieve into a bowl. Cool completely and then refrigerate until needed. This keeps in the fridge for up to a week.

CASHEW VANILLA FROSTING

Makes enough frosting to sandwich a 20cm cake together or top 12 cupcakes. Make double if you want to both fill and cover a cake with the frosting.

Prep time: 20–25 minutes, including soaking time

This light and fluffy, easy-to-make cashew nut frosting can be used as a cake filling, cupcake topping or as an alternative icing for the Carrot Cake (see recipe on p. 93)

INGREDIENTS

120g cashew nuts

40ml maple syrup

1 teaspoon vanilla extract

2 teaspoons fresh lemon juice

METHOD

Place the cashew nuts in a pan, cover them with boiling water and set aside to soak for at least 15 minutes. Next, drain off the water. Add the softened nuts to the nut grinder attachment of a food processor with the remaining ingredients and blitz until smooth and creamy, stopping and scraping down the sides with a spatula if needed. Transfer to a bowl or jug, cover, and keep in the fridge until needed. Use within two days.

CHEESECAKE BASE 1 (DIGESTIVES)

Makes sufficient to cover a 20cm round baking tin

Prep time: 10 minutes

This is the classic cheesecake base that most will have used at some time, using crushed biscuits and, in this case, melted vegan butter.

INGREDIENTS

200g vegan digestive biscuits or vegan gingernuts

1 teaspoon ground ginger (optional, if using digestive biscuits)

75g soft vegan butter (such as Vitalite) + extra for greasing

METHOD

Lightly grease a 20cm round spring-form baking tin or a glass pie dish.

Crush the biscuits in a plastic bag with a rolling pin until you have large crumbs. Add the ground ginger to the biscuit crumbs in the bag at this stage if using.

Tip ... using a re-usable zip-lock plastic bag for crushing the biscuits makes it so much easier. Leave the bag slightly open to let air pass through. Melt the vegan butter in a saucepan then stir in the biscuit crumbs. Tip the mixture into the baking tin or dish, and spread evenly and firmly over the base – you want the base to be compacted. Chill in the fridge while you make the cheesecake topping.

CHEESECAKE BASE 2 (NUTS AND DATES)

Makes enough to cover a 20cm round baking tin

Prep time: 15 minutes

This base, made from nuts and dates, provides a delicious, healthier alternative to using crushed biscuits.

INGREDIENTS

2 tablespoons cocoa powder

100g pitted soft or Medjool dates

50g unblanched hazelnuts

150g unblanched almonds

A pinch of salt

2 tablespoons coconut butter, melted at room temperature

METHOD

Lightly grease the base of a round 20cm spring form cake tin or glass pie dish and then dust 1 tablespoon of the cocoa powder evenly over the base.

Place the dates in a small bowl, cover with boiling water, soak for 10 minutes, then discard the water.

Blitz the hazelnuts and almonds in the nut or coffee grinder of a food processor. Then add the softened dates, the remaining tablespoon of cocoa powder, the salt and the melted coconut butter and pulse, then blitz into a dough. Place in the prepared cake tin or glass dish, tamp down evenly with the back of a spoon and chill until needed.

CHOCOLATE GANACHE

Makes enough to cover a 20cm cake

Prep time: 10 minutes

This is an indulgent chocolate ganache which is used to top my Chocolate, Beetroot and Cardamom Cake (see recipe on p. 94). It also makes a velvety smooth filling for a vanilla sponge cake, a coffee cake or as a frosting for cupcakes.

INGREDIENTS

150g vegan dark chocolate (at least 54% cocoa solids), broken into pieces

150ml soya cream

1 teaspoon dark muscovado or dark brown sugar

1½ teaspoons coconut butter

METHOD

Put the chocolate in a heat-proof bowl and set aside.

Add the soya cream and sugar to a saucepan and heat until boiling point. Pour the cream mixture over the chocolate and allow it to stand for 5 minutes. Then add the coconut butter and stir until well-combined and glossy. Allow the ganache to cool a little, but not set, before using.

COFFEE BUTTERCREAM

Makes enough to fill and cover a 20cm cake

Prep time: 5 minutes

This rich buttercream accompanies the recipe for Coffee Cake (see p. 98), and can also be used as a topping on cupcakes or coffee buns.

INGREDIENTS

100g soft vegan butter (such as Vitalite)

200g icing sugar

1 tablespoon espresso powder mixed with 1 teaspoon boiling water

METHOD

Cream the butter with a fork in a bowl. Gradually stir in the icing sugar until you have a thick buttercream. Then stir in the espresso a little at a time. Refrigerate until needed. This will keep for 2–3 days in the fridge.

CREAM CHEESE FROSTING

Makes enough to cover a 20cm cake

Prep time: 5–10 minutes

This frosting is for topping my Carrot Cake (see recipe on p. 93), although it can also be used as a frosting for cupcakes or muffins, or to fill a vanilla sponge cake or walnut cake.

INGREDIENTS

100g vegan cream cheese (such as Violife)

100g icing sugar

1 teaspoon vanilla extract

1 teaspoon lemon juice

METHOD

Cream together the vegan cream cheese and the icing sugar with a fork until well mixed. Stir in the vanilla extract and the lemon juice. Refrigerate before using. The frosting will keep for a day in the fridge.

GINGERBREAD BUTTERCREAM

Makes enough to fill and cover a 20cm cake

Prep time: 5 minutes

This buttercream accompanies the recipe for Pear and Ginger Cake (see p. 110) and can also be used as a topping on cupcakes or as a filling for a vanilla sponge cake.

INGREDIENTS

100g soft vegan butter (such as Vitalite)

200g icing sugar

1½ pieces of stem ginger in syrup, chopped finely.

METHOD

Cream the butter with a fork in a bowl. Gradually stir in the icing sugar until you have a thick buttercream. Then stir in the stem ginger pieces. Refrigerate until needed. This will keep for 2–3 days in the fridge.

A word about . . . ginger

Ginger contains gingerol, which is its main bioactive compound. Gingerol has anti-inflammatory and antioxidant properties. It also contains reasonable amounts of potassium.

LEMON CURD

Makes around 225ml

Prep time: 10 minutes

This vegan lemon curd is a filling for the Lemon Curd Tarts (see recipe on p. 183) as well as for the Coconut and Lemon Cake (see recipe on p. 97). It is also delicious as a filling for a lemon meringue pie.

INGREDIENTS

4 tablespoons cornflour

3 tablespoons cold water

50ml lemon juice (around 2 small lemons)

125g caster sugar

30g vegan butter (block butter is best, such as Naturli)

METHOD

Mix the cornflour and water together in a cup to make a runny paste. Set aside.

Add the lemon juice and sugar to a pan and bring to boiling point. Then add the cornflour mixture and stir continuously until the curd thickens.

Remove from the heat and stir in the vegan butter. Pour into a glass jar and leave to cool completely before sealing with a lid and refrigerating until needed. Best used within a week or so of making.

A word about . . . lemons

Lemons are very high in Vitamin C – a lemon contains about half the recommended daily amount of the vitamin. They also contain fibre, and have heart-protecting qualities as well as helping to lower cholesterol. They also help promote the uptake of iron from plant-based foods. Try a hot lemon drink (juice and pulp) sweetened with a little vegan honey for an alternative to tea and coffee.

LEMON ICING

Makes enough to drizzle over a 20cm cake or over 12 small buns

Prep time: 5 minutes

This simple lemon icing accompanies the Pistachio and Lemon Square Cake (see recipe on p. 113) and can also be used as a drizzle for cupcakes, buns, muffins or a lemon drizzle cake.

INGREDIENTS

50g icing sugar

Freshly squeezed lemon juice (about 2 teaspoons)

METHOD

Place the icing sugar in a bowl and gradually stir in enough lemon juice until you have a thick and just pourable glaze which you can drizzle over your cooled cake, buns or cupcakes. If the icing is too runny, add a little more icing sugar to bring it to the consistency you need and add more lemon juice, a little at a time, if the icing is too thick.

MARMALADE GLAZE

Makes enough to cover an 18–20cm cake

Prep time: 5 minutes

Cooking time: 10 minutes

This glaze provides the topping for the Marmalade Cake recipe (see p. 109) although it can also be used on other cakes or baked goods. It has a lovely sweet-sharp citrusy flavour which offsets a cake's sweetness.

INGREDIENTS

1½ tablespoons orange marmalade

Juice and zest of 1 orange

3 tablespoons soft brown sugar

METHOD

Stir the marmalade, orange juice, orange zest and sugar together in a pan. Bring the mixture to boiling point then keep on a rolling boil until a syrup forms. Set aside to cool before spreading over your cake, cupcakes, buns or muffins.

PECAN CRUMBLE TOPPING

{Can be prepared in advance and set aside somewhere cool for 24 hours}

Makes enough to cover a 20cm pie dish

Prep time: 15 minutes

This crumble topping can be used with any fruit as a dessert, although is used in this book in combination with apple and a pastry tart case for my Apple Pecan Crumble Tart (see recipe on p. 139).

INGREDIENTS

200g plain white flour

A pinch of salt

100g vegan butter (block butter is best, such as Naturli)

50g demerara sugar

40g pecans, chopped roughly

METHOD

Add the flour and salt to a mixing bowl. Cut the butter into the flour and then rub it in with your fingers until the mixture resembles coarse breadcrumbs. Stir in the demerara sugar and chopped pecans and set aside until needed.

SALTED DATE CARAMEL

Makes around 250g

Prep time: 5 minutes

Cooking time: 8–10 minutes

I use this caramel in my Banana and Salted Date Caramel Slices (see recipe on p. 153) although it could also be used as a filling or topping for a chocolate cake or as a frosting for cupcakes and muffins.

INGREDIENTS

150g pitted Medjool or other soft dates

180ml boiling water

¼ teaspoon flaked sea salt

1 teaspoon vanilla extract

2 teaspoons almond butter

METHOD

Put all of the ingredients in a blender jug and pulse first a few times and then process until the caramel is silky smooth. You will need to stop and scrape down the sides of the blender several times to ensure the mixture is smooth.

Taste and add more salt or vanilla if required. Refrigerate until ready to use. This will keep in the fridge for at least two weeks.

A word about . . . dates

Dried dates are a good source of energy, natural sugar, fibre and various minerals including calcium, copper, iron, magnesium, phosphorus, potassium, sodium and zinc. They also contain important vitamins such as vitamin A, vitamin B6, vitamin K, folate, niacin, riboflavin and thiamine.

STRAWBERRY AND ELDERFLOWER CHIA JAM

Makes approximately 240g

Prep time: 5 minutes + setting and cooling time

Cooking time: 5–6 minutes

This jam contains very little sugar – just some elderflower syrup. It uses the magical property of highly nutritious chia seeds to thicken the preserve.

INGREDIENTS

200g fresh hulled strawberries, chopped roughly

3 tablespoons elderflower syrup

½ teaspoon vanilla extract

2 tablespoons ground chia seeds

METHOD

Place the strawberries, elderflower syrup and vanilla extract in a medium saucepan. Bring to a medium heat, then turn down the heat once the juices are being released from the strawberries and cook for 5 or 6 minutes until the strawberries have broken down. Remove from the heat and mash with the back of a spoon until the fruit forms a soft pulp with some bits of strawberry still in it.

Set aside to cool. Taste and stir in a little more elderflower syrup if you want more sweetness and then stir in the chia seeds. Transfer the jam to a covered bowl or jam jar with a sealed lid and chill in the fridge until needed. The jam will keep in the fridge for at least two weeks.

A word about . . . chia seeds

Chia seeds have many benefits as they contain protein, fibre and antioxidants, and are also a source of minerals including calcium, magnesium and phosphorous. Chia seeds expand when mixed with liquid and can be used to thicken mousses, smoothies, cakes and brownies in the same way that flax seeds are used in baking.

SWEET DATE AND NUT TART CASE

Makes 1 standard tart case or 8–12 small tart cases

Prep time: 10 minutes

I like to have a no-bake option for pastry that uses an alternative to flour and contains natural fruit sugars. This no-bake tart case is an ideal base for any number of fillings including fruit purée, Lemon Curd (see the recipe on p. 31) or Chocolate Ganache (see the recipe on p. 26).

INGREDIENTS

100g whole, unblanched almonds

100g shelled walnuts

5 stoned Medjool or soft dates, chopped roughly (about 100g)

2 tablespoons crunchy peanut butter

METHOD

In the bowl of a food processor place all of the ingredients and pulse about a dozen times, and then whizz until the mixture clumps together. Next, spoon the mixture into your tart case and press into the base and sides with the back of a spoon or spoon walnut sized pieces into your mini tart cases and press into the base and sides to form small hollows for your filling. Chill until needed.

SWEET SHORTCRUST PASTRY

{Can be prepared in advance}

Makes enough pastry to line 2 x 20cm tart cases

Prep time: 10 minutes + chilling time

Cooking time: 25–30 minutes

Everyone needs a recipe for a vegan shortcrust pastry – it's so versatile, simple to make and a classic! You can use shortcrust pastry for all kinds of tarts and sweet pies.

INGREDIENTS

250g plain white flour

25g ground almonds

A pinch of salt

100g fridge-cold vegan butter block (such as Naturli)

25g caster sugar

Cold water as needed

METHOD

Combine the flour, ground almonds and salt in a bowl. Cut in the vegan butter and then rub it into the flour with your fingertips until it resembles coarse breadcrumbs. Stir in the sugar. Add a few drops of cold water at a time and, with your hands, bring the mixture together into a firm ball. Work quickly in order to keep the pastry as cool as possible.

Tip … if you add too much water you can add more flour to bring the pastry to the right consistency. Wrap the pastry in cling film and chill in the fridge for at least 30 minutes (you can also make the pastry in advance and keep it overnight in the fridge).

Heat the oven to 180°C.

To make a tart case, lightly flour a rolling pin and roll the pastry out on a lightly floured, cold surface to around 3–4mm thickness, to a size several centimetres larger than your tart case. Roll the pastry onto the rolling pin and lift it over the tart case, pressing it into the bottom of the case and around the sides. Trim off the excess pastry and prick the bottom of the tart all over with a fork (this will allow steam to be released from the pastry and avoid a 'soggy bottom').

Next, line the tart case with greaseproof baking paper and fill it with baking beans (this will prevent the pastry from puffing up). If you don't have baking beans you can use dried rice, dried lentils or dried chickpeas instead. Bake in the preheated oven for 15 minutes (i.e. 'blind') then take the tart case out of the oven, remove the beans (or alternative if using) and greaseproof baking paper and return it to the oven to cook for a further 10–15 minutes or until the pastry is golden. Remove from the oven and allow to cool before adding a cold filling.

WHIPPED CREAM

{Prepare in advance}

Makes around 150ml

Prep time: 5 minutes

There are a few whipping creams now available commercially, but this recipe allows you to whip one up from scratch! I use this cream in my Victoria Sponge recipe (see p. 118). I also serve it with scones and with fruit pies, tarts, crumbles and trifle.

INGREDIENTS

150ml from a 250ml chilled carton of coconut cream (not creamed coconut or coconut milk)

1 tablespoon icing sugar

½ teaspoon vanilla extract

METHOD

Put the coconut cream, icing sugar and vanilla extract in a bowl and stir to combine. Refrigerate until needed. This will keep for 2–3 days in the fridge.

1

BISCUITS

ABERNETHY BISCUITS

Makes 24 biscuits

Prep time: 15 minutes + chilling time

Cooking time: 16–18 minutes

These biscuits are associated with a nineteenth-century Scottish doctor, John Abernethy, who had connections to the Perthshire town. He is said to have suggested to his local baker that adding caraway seeds and sugar to plain biscuits would aid digestion.

INGREDIENTS

180g plain white flour or plain wholemeal flour

90g vegan butter (block butter is best, such as Naturli)

60g demerara sugar

2 teaspoons caraway seeds

A pinch of salt

Soya milk or other plant milk to bind

A little caster sugar for sprinkling

METHOD

Line a baking tray with greaseproof baking paper.

Place the flour and butter in a bowl and cut the butter into the flour, then rub it in with your fingertips until the mixture resembles breadcrumbs. Next stir in the sugar, caraway seeds and salt. Adding a few drops of soya milk at a time, bring the mixture together into a fairly stiff ball of dough. Wrap the dough in cling film and chill in the fridge for 30 minutes.

Heat the oven to 190°C.

Roll out the dough on a floured surface to around 3–4mm thick, then cut out circles with a 6cm round biscuit cutter or with cutters of your choice. Re-roll and cut out the remaining dough until it has all been used. Prick the surface of each biscuit with a fork a few times, place on the baking tray and bake for 16–18 minutes. Once cooked, sprinkle with a little caster sugar and transfer the biscuits to a wire rack to cool completely. These will keep in an airtight container for a week or so.

DIGESTIVE BISCUITS

Makes around 18 biscuits

Prep time: 15 minutes + chilling time

Cooking time: 20 minutes

Who doesn't like a digestive biscuit dunked in a cup of tea? Digestive biscuits hail from Scotland, and were invented in 1839 by two Scottish doctors as an aid to digestion (said to derive from the use of bicarbonate of soda in the recipe). In 1892, Alexander Grant developed and patented the original recipe for McVitie's digestive biscuits. The distinctive flavour comes from using brown wheat flour and malt extract. This recipe uses a combination of wheat flour and oatmeal.

INGREDIENTS

200g wholemeal plain flour

100g medium oatmeal or pinhead oatmeal

70g soft brown or demerara sugar

½ teaspoon bicarbonate of soda

¼ teaspoon salt

100g vegan butter (block butter is best, such as Naturli)

Soya milk or other plant milk to bind

METHOD

Line 2 rectangular trays with greaseproof baking paper.

Mix the flour, oatmeal, sugar, bicarbonate of soda and salt together in a bowl. Cut the butter into the flour mixture, then rub it in with your fingertips until it resembles coarse breadcrumbs. Adding a few drops of soya milk at a time, bring the mixture together into a fairly stiff ball of dough. Wrap the dough in cling film and chill in the fridge for 30 minutes.

Heat the oven to 190°C.

Roll out the dough on a floured surface to around 3–4 mm thick, then cut out the digestives with a 7cm biscuit cutter or cutter of your choice and place them on the trays, leaving a little room around the edges for the biscuits to expand. Prick each biscuit all over with a fork. Re-roll and repeat the process with the remaining dough.

Bake for 20 minutes or until firm, then transfer the biscuits to a wire rack to cool completely. They will keep for up to a week in an airtight container.

EMPIRE BISCUITS

Makes 10 biscuits

Prep time: 15 minutes + chilling time

Cooking time: 15 minutes

You may see Empire biscuits called Linzer biscuits or German biscuits. With the outbreak of the First World War, they were renamed Empire biscuits in England and Belgian biscuits in Scotland because Belgium had just been invaded. However, they are also known simply as Scottish Iced Cookies. They are a very sweet and delicious treat using a double layer of thick shortcake sandwiched together with jam and topped with white icing and a glacé cherry (or a sweetie such as a vegan jelly tot).

INGREDIENTS

125g soft vegan butter (such as Vitalite)

100g caster sugar

1 teaspoon vanilla extract

1 tablespoon vegan sweetened condensed milk

300g plain white flour

A pinch of salt

Soya milk or other plant milk to bind

METHOD

Line a rectangular baking sheet with greaseproof baking paper.

Cream the butter and sugar together in a bowl. Stir in the vanilla extract and the vegan condensed milk. Add the flour and salt and mix with a fork. Add a few drops of soya milk at a time and bring everything together with your hands to form a stiff dough. Wrap the dough in cling film and chill for 30 minutes.

Heat the oven to 190°C.

Roll out the dough on a floured surface to around 3mm thick. Cut out 20 circles with a 7cm biscuit cutter or a cutter of your choice and place on the baking sheet. Re-roll and cut out the remaining dough.

Bake for 15 minutes or until golden. Then transfer the biscuits to a wire rack to cool completely.

To Assemble the Biscuits

9–10 teaspoons high fruit content strawberry jam or Strawberry and Elderflower Chia Jam (see recipe on p. 37)

100g icing sugar

Cold water as needed

5 glacé cherries, halved

Sandwich the biscuits together with a teaspoon of jam and place on a plate.

Put the icing sugar in a bowl and stir in enough cold water, a little at a time, to make a thick icing. Spread the icing over the top of each biscuit and top with half a glacé cherry. Transfer to an airtight container until needed where they will keep for 3–4 days.

GINGERBREAD HEARTS

Makes about 14–16 large hearts or 24 small hearts

Prep time: 10 minutes + chilling time

Cooking time: 12–14 minutes

A slightly different take on gingerbread people, these are gingerbread hearts, which are sometimes iced, although I prefer them plain. They are delicious with a cup of tea. If you prefer to make gingerbread figures or other shapes, the mixture works just the same.

INGREDIENTS

340g plain wholemeal or plain white flour

1 teaspoon bicarbonate of soda

1½ teaspoons ground ginger

½ teaspoon ground mixed spice

110g soft vegan butter (such as Vitalite)

110g dark brown or muscovado sugar

2 tablespoons black treacle

1 tablespoon golden syrup

METHOD

Heat the oven to 180°C and grease and line 2 rectangular baking sheets with greaseproof baking paper.

Combine the flour, bicarbonate of soda, ginger and mixed spice in a mixing bowl. Place the butter, sugar, treacle and golden syrup in a saucepan on low-medium heat to melt. Remove from the heat and cool for 5 minutes then stir into the flour mixture. With a spoon and then with your hands bring everything together into a soft ball of dough. Wrap in cling film and chill in the fridge for 30 minutes.

On a floured surface with a lightly floured rolling pin, roll out the dough to around 2.5cm thick. Cut out your heart shapes with your biscuit cutter and place on the prepared baking sheets. Re-roll and cut out the remaining dough. Bake in the oven for around 12–14 minutes until golden brown and firm. Remove from the oven and transfer to a wire rack to cool completely. These will keep for a week or so in an airtight container.

GINGER OATIES

Makes 10–12

Prep time: 10 minutes

Cooking time: 15 minutes

These ginger oaties are a Scottish take on a chewier kind of American-style cookie and are made, as the name suggests, with oats. They are simple to make and are the ideal accompaniment to a soothing hot drink and a sit down.

INGREDIENTS

100g wholemeal self-raising flour (or 100g wholemeal plain flour + 1½ teaspoons baking powder)

75g porridge oats

50g demerara or soft brown sugar

½ teaspoon bicarbonate of soda

1 teaspoon ground ginger

A pinch of salt

60g soft vegan butter (such as Vitalite)

3 tablespoons black treacle

METHOD

Heat the oven to 180°C. Line a baking tray with greaseproof baking paper.

Mix the flour, oats, sugar, bicarbonate of soda, ground ginger and salt together in a bowl. Make a well in the middle of the mixture. Set aside. Melt the vegan butter and treacle together in a pan (do not allow to boil).

Pour the wet ingredients into the dry ingredients and bring everything together to form a ball of sticky dough. Break off pieces of the dough, and shape into a ball about the size of a walnut. Place on the baking tray. Continue this process until all the mixture has been used. Flatten each ball with your fingers leaving space between for the biscuits to spread when cooking.

Bake in the oven for 15 minutes. Remove from the oven and leave to sit on the tray for 5 minutes before transferring to a wire rack to cool completely. The oaties will keep in an airtight container for 3–4 days.

MONTROSE TEACAKES

Makes 12

Prep time: 15 minutes

Cooking time: 25 minutes

These little teacakes may be named after the town of Montrose on the north-east coast of Scotland, or after James Graham, the First Marquess of Montrose. Or perhaps both. Either way, they are tasty treats and have a delicate flavour of rose water.

INGREDIENTS

60ml soya milk

1 teaspoon apple cider vinegar

60g raisins

1 tablespoon vegan brandy

115g white or wholemeal self-raising flour

40g rice flour or brown rice flour

½ teaspoon baking powder

¼ teaspoon bicarbonate of soda

¼ teaspoon ground nutmeg

55g soft brown sugar

A pinch of salt

55ml sunflower oil or olive oil

50ml water

¼ teaspoon rose water

METHOD

Line a 12-hole muffin tray with paper cases. Heat the oven to 180°C.

Combine the soya milk and apple cider vinegar in a jug and set aside to curdle and form vegan buttermilk.

Put the raisins in a bowl, add the brandy and set aside.

Place both kinds of flour, baking powder, bicarbonate of soda, nutmeg, sugar and salt in a bowl and combine. Add the buttermilk, oil and water and mix gently together. Then stir in the rose water and the raisins.

Spoon the mixture evenly into the paper cases – an ice cream scoop can help here. Then bake for 25 minutes or until risen and golden.

Remove from the oven and transfer to a wire rack to cool completely. These will keep for 2–3 days in an airtight container.

PAISLEY ALMOND CAKES

Makes 9 small cakes

Prep time: 15 minutes

Cooking time: 25–30 minutes

Paisley, the largest town in the Scottish county of Renfrewshire, just west of Glasgow, was once known for its handloom weaving among other things. These moreish little cakes originally contained rice flour and eggs, although I have substituted self-raising flour to help bind the cakes and allow them to rise.

INGREDIENTS

60ml unsweetened soya milk

1 teaspoon apple cider vinegar

150g white or wholemeal self-raising flour

½ teaspoon bicarbonate of soda

55g caster sugar

A pinch of salt

55ml olive oil or sunflower oil

50ml water

1½ teaspoons almond extract

Flaked almonds to sprinkle

METHOD

Heat the oven to 180°C. Line a 12–hole cupcake tin with 9 paper cases.

Mix the soya milk and the apple cider vinegar together in a cup and set aside for a few minutes to form vegan buttermilk.

Combine the flour, bicarbonate of soda, sugar and salt in a bowl. Next, add the vegan buttermilk, oil, water and almond extract to the flour mixture and stir gently to make the batter.

Half-fill each cupcake case with the batter mixture (an ice cream scoop can help here), then sprinkle flaked almonds on top. Bake in the oven for 25–30 minutes or until risen and golden brown.

Remove from the oven and transfer to a wire rack to cool completely. These will keep for 2–3 days in an airtight container.

SHORTBREAD

Makes about 14–16 biscuits

Prep time: 15 minutes

Cooking time: 25–30 minutes

Shortbread is synonymous with Scottish baking, so I have provided several recipe options. Traditionally, shortbread follows a ratio of 3:2:1 of flour to fat to sugar, and most recipes will work from such a base.

Cooking times for shortbread depend a little on how thin or chunky you roll out your dough and whether or not you have added cream.

Ayrshire Shortbread

In Ayrshire, shortbread is an altogether richer fare than a standard shortbread, with the addition of cream to the usual trinity of butter, sugar and flour, and it has a softer texture. This vegan version uses oat cream, but you could also use soya or any other plant-based cream.

INGREDIENTS

100g soft vegan butter (such as Vitalite)

50g caster sugar + extra for sprinkling

2 tablespoons oat cream

180g–190g plain white flour

METHOD

Heat the oven to 180°C. Line a baking tray with greaseproof baking paper.

Cream the vegan butter and sugar together in a bowl. Stir in the cream and the flour and bring the mixture together with your hands to form a soft dough. Roll out the dough on a lightly floured worktop until around 3mm thick. Then cut out the shapes you would like with a biscuit cutter or cut into traditional rectangular fingers. Re-roll and cut out the remaining dough.

Transfer the shortbread onto the baking tray, then lightly prick the surface of each shape with a fork. Bake in the oven for around 25–30 minutes or until the shortbread is golden in colour. Remove from the oven and sprinkle the biscuits with a little caster sugar. Cool for 5 minutes then transfer to a wire rack to cool completely. These will keep in an airtight container for 2–3 days.

GLUTEN-FREE SHORTBREAD

Makes about 16 star shapes

Prep time: 15 minutes

Cooking time: 20 minutes

This is one of my favourite shortbreads; it has both a crunch and a melt-in-the-mouth quality. I use rice flour, ground almonds and cornflour to make this recipe both vegan and gluten-free.

INGREDIENTS

100g soft vegan butter (such as Vitalite)

50g caster sugar + extra for sprinkling

80g rice flour or brown rice flour

50g ground almonds

50g cornflour

METHOD

Heat the oven to 180°C. Line a baking tray with greaseproof baking paper.

Cream the butter and sugar together. Add the rice flour, ground almonds and cornflour and, with your hands, bring the mixture together to form a soft dough. Roll out the dough on a worktop lightly dusted with rice flour until around 3mm thick. Then cut out the shapes you would like with a biscuit cutter. Re-roll and cut out the remaining dough.

Transfer the shortbread onto the baking tray, then lightly prick the surface of each shape with a fork. Bake in the oven for around 20 minutes or until the shortbread is golden in colour. If you use brown rice flour the shortbread will be darker in colour.

Remove from the oven and sprinkle the biscuits with a little caster sugar. Cool for 5 minutes then transfer to a wire rack to cool completely. These will keep in an airtight container for 2–3 days.

PETTICOAT TAILS

Makes 1 round shortbread / 8 biscuits

Prep time: 15 minutes

Cooking time: 40–45 minutes

These are triangular shaped shortbreads, baked in a single circle. They need a little more cooking time given they are in a round, and because I use icing sugar in this recipe, they need a little more flour than usual.

INGREDIENTS

100g soft vegan butter (such as Vitalite)

50g icing sugar

180g plain white flour

Caster sugar for dusting

METHOD

Heat the oven to 180°C. Line a 20cm round baking tin with greaseproof baking paper.

Cream the vegan butter and icing sugar together in a bowl. Stir in the flour and bring the mixture together with your hands to form a soft dough. Press the dough into the baking tin, leaving thumb prints round the edge, and score into 8 triangles. Lightly prick the surface with a fork and bake in the oven for around 40–45 minutes or until the shortbread is golden in colour.

Remove from the oven and sprinkle with a little caster sugar. Cool for 5 minutes then transfer to a wire rack to cool completely before breaking apart into the triangles. These will keep in an airtight container for 2–3 days.

PITCAITHLY BANNOCK

Makes 18–20 biscuits

Prep time: 15 minutes

Cooking time: 25–30 minutes

A Pitcaithly Bannock is a shortbread that comes from the town of Pitcaithly in Perthshire. Traditionally it is made from plain flour, rice flour, sugar, butter, almonds and candied lemon peel and I have followed this replacing white sugar with demerara sugar and butter with vegan butter. If you cannot come by candied lemon peel, you can use candied mixed peel.

INGREDIENTS

100g soft vegan butter (such as Vitalite)

50g demerara sugar

100g plain white flour

50g rice flour or brown rice flour

25g blanched flaked almonds

1 tablespoon candied lemon peel, chopped finely

Caster sugar for sprinkling

METHOD

Heat the oven to 180°C. Line a larger rectangular baking tray with greaseproof baking paper.

Cream the vegan butter and sugar together in a bowl. Stir in the flour, rice flour, flaked almonds and lemon peel and bring the mixture together with your hands to form a soft dough. Roll out the dough on a lightly dusted worktop until around 3mm thick. Then cut out the shapes you would like with a biscuit cutter. Re-roll and cut out the remaining dough.

Transfer the shortbread onto the baking tray, then lightly prick the surface of each shape with a fork. Bake in the oven for around 25–30 minutes or until the shortbread is golden in colour. If you use brown rice flour the shortbread will be darker in colour.

Remove from the oven and sprinkle the biscuits with a little caster sugar. Cool for 5 minutes then transfer to a wire rack to cool completely. These will keep in an airtight container for 2–3 days.

PLAIN SHORTBREAD

Makes 18–20 biscuits

Prep time: 15 minutes

Cooking time: 20 minutes

This recipe for shortbread includes polenta which provides an extra crunch. Semolina can also be used instead of polenta. The combination of the polenta/semolina with demerara sugar really makes this shortbread stand out.

INGREDIENTS

100g soft vegan butter (such as Vitalite)

50g demerara sugar (or caster sugar) + extra for sprinkling

100g plain white flour

50g polenta or semolina

METHOD

Line a baking tray with greaseproof baking paper. Heat the oven to 180°C.

Cream the vegan butter and sugar together in a bowl. Stir in the flour and polenta and bring the mixture together with your hands to form a soft dough. Roll out the dough on a lightly dusted worktop until around 3mm thick. Then cut out the shapes you would like with a biscuit cutter or cut into traditional rectangular 'fingers'. Re-roll and cut out the remaining dough.

Transfer the shortbread onto the baking tray, then lightly prick the surface of each shape with a fork. Bake in the oven for around 20 minutes or until the shortbread is golden in colour.

Remove from the oven and sprinkle the biscuits with a little demerara or caster sugar. Cool for 5 minutes then transfer to a wire rack to cool completely. These will keep in an airtight container for 2–3 days.

SHETLAND BRIDE'S CAKE

Makes 8 pieces

Prep time: 10 minutes

Cooking time: 40–45 minutes

This Shetland shortbread is also known as Bride's Bun/Bonn or Dreaming Cake, and is a cross between a biscuit and a scone. Traditionally it was cooked on a griddle or girdle by the mother of the bride. It is said that the 'cake' was broken over the head of the bride as she crossed the threshold of the marital home following her wedding and collected by those seeking romance who would keep the shortbread under their pillows and 'dream' about a beloved one.

INGREDIENTS

100g soft vegan butter (such as Vitalite)

50g demerara sugar or caster sugar + extra for sprinkling

150g plain white flour

1 teaspoon caraway seeds

METHOD

Heat the oven to 180°C. Line a baking tray with greaseproof baking paper.

Cream the vegan butter and sugar together in a bowl. Stir in the flour and caraway seeds and then bring the mixture together with your hands to form a soft dough.

Roll out the dough on a floured surface to around 18cm in diameter then place it on the baking tray, prick the surface with a fork and score into 8 triangular pieces. Bake for around 40–45 minutes or until golden brown. Remove from the oven and sprinkle with demerara or caster sugar. Cool on the tray for 5 minutes, then transfer to a wire rack to cool completely. To serve, break into 8 triangles. The shortbread will keep in an airtight container for 2–3 days.

TANTALLON CAKES

Makes 16 biscuits

Prep time: 15 minutes

Cooking time: 20–25 minutes

More like shortbread than a cake, these biscuits are associated with Tantallon Castle in East Lothian near Edinburgh. They go well with a nice cup of jasmine or fruit tea.

INGREDIENTS

100g vegan butter (such as Vitalite)

50g caster sugar

Zest of 1 unwaxed lemon

1 heaped tablespoon lemon marmalade or mixed fruit marmalade (such as orange, grapefruit and lemon)

100g plain white flour

50g rice flour

Demerara sugar for sprinkling

METHOD

Heat the oven to 170°C. Line a baking tray with greaseproof baking paper.

Cream the vegan butter and sugar together then fold in the lemon zest and marmalade. Add the two types of flour and bring the mixture together with your hands to form a dough.

Roll out the dough on a floured board to around 4–5mm and then cut out rounds with a 6cm pastry cutter and place them on the baking tray. Re-roll and cut out any leftover dough until you have used it all.

Prick the top of the dough with a fork and then bake for 20–25 minutes until golden, covering if starting to brown. Remove from the oven and sprinkle with a little demerara sugar. Cool on the tray for 5 minutes then place on a wire rack to cool completely. These will keep in an airtight container for 2–3 days.

2

BREAD, BUNS, OATCAKES AND FRUIT LOAVES

BANNOCKS

Makes 4 bannocks

Prep time: 10–15 minutes

Cooking time: 20–25 minutes

Traditionally bannocks were eaten in the Scottish Highlands and were cooked on a griddle or girdle. You can add any grain: barley meal, fine or pinhead oatmeal, oat flour (either buy or you can make your own by whizzing porridge oats in a food processor) or Orkney beremeal. I use fine oatmeal. Bannocks are delicious served with vegan butter and jam, with vegan cream cheese and marmalade or as an accompaniment to soups and casseroles.

INGREDIENTS

100ml soya milk or oat milk

1 teaspoon apple cider vinegar

125g strong white bread flour + extra for sprinkling

50g wholemeal self-raising flour

50g oatmeal

1 teaspoon bicarbonate of soda

¼ teaspoon salt

METHOD

Line a baking tray with greaseproof baking paper. Heat the oven to 190°C.

Combine the soya milk or oat milk with the apple cider vinegar in a jug and set aside to curdle into vegan buttermilk.

Mix the two types of flour, oatmeal, bicarbonate of soda and salt together in a bowl. Make a well in the middle of the flour mixture and stir in the vegan buttermilk, bringing everything together with your hands until you have a ball of dough.

Dust your work surface with flour and shape the dough into a circle around 20cm in diameter. Cut the circle into four triangles (known as 'farls'), place on the baking tray and bake for 20–25 minutes. Transfer to a wire rack to cool or serve warm. The bannocks are best eaten the day they are made.

BAPS – BREAKFAST ROLLS

Makes 6 baps

Prep time: 15 minutes + 45–60 minutes rising + 20–30 minutes proving

Cooking time: 10–12 minutes

A bap is a soft white floury bread roll or morning roll that originates in Scotland, and is traditionally made with a combination of flour, milk, sugar, salt, yeast and fat. Baps generally contain a savoury filling and can be filled with vegan sausages or burgers. If you want to take the sweet option, spread with vegan butter and your favourite jam or marmalade.

You can also substitute strong wholemeal bread flour in this recipe if preferred.

INGREDIENTS

300g strong white bread flour + extra for kneading and dusting

25g vegan butter (block butter is best, such as Naturli)

1 x 7g sachet easy bake dried yeast

1 teaspoon caster sugar

1 teaspoon salt

45ml soya milk or oat milk at room temperature + extra for brushing

150ml tepid water

METHOD

Line a baking tray with greaseproof baking paper and dust with flour.

Put the flour in a bowl and cut the vegan butter in with a knife, then rub it between your fingers until it resembles breadcrumbs. Stir in the yeast, sugar and salt.

Add the milk and water to the flour mixture and bring everything together with your hands to form a soft dough.

Knead the dough on a surface dusted with flour for around 5–7 minutes. Lightly oil a bowl and put the dough in it, cover with cling film or a clean tea towel, and leave in a warm place for 45–60 minutes to rise, or until the dough has doubled in size.

Knock (punch) back the dough. Then divide it into 6 equal pieces and shape each into a round. Press your thumb into the middle of each roll (this prevents a crust from forming), place the baps on the floured baking sheet, cover and prove for 20–30 minutes in a warm place until well risen. Then brush the baps with a little soya milk or oat milk and sprinkle a little flour over them.

Heat the oven to 220°C then bake the baps for 10–12 minutes until a light golden brown. The baps are done if they sound hollow when tapped on the base. Transfer to a wire rack and sprinkle again with flour.

Eat warm, or allow to cool before filling. These are best eaten the day they are made although they can be re-heated in the oven.

BARM (FERMENTED) LOAF

Makes 1 large loaf

Prep time: 15 minutes + 60 minutes rising + 45–60 minutes proving

Cooking time: 25–30 minutes

A barm loaf is traditionally made with oatmeal, the yeasty froth on the top of fermented ale, called the barm, and treacle, and it is baked in an oven. In Scotland it was often eaten at peat-cutting time. Given the addition of beer and treacle, a fermented barm loaf has a sweet taste compared to, for example, a sourdough.

INGREDIENTS

150ml dark organic beer (e.g. Black Isle Organic Wheat Beer, Black Wolf, Barney's Red Rye Beer or Dark Island Dark Ale) at room temperature

175ml warm water

1 tablespoon black treacle

250g strong white bread flour + extra for kneading

150g rye flour

100g fine or pinhead oatmeal

1 x 7g packet easy bake dried yeast

1½ teaspoons salt

METHOD

Line a rectangular baking tray with greaseproof baking paper.

Stir together the beer, water and treacle in a jug and set aside.

Combine the two types of flour, the oatmeal, yeast and salt in a mixing bowl. Add the beer mixture and bring everything together with your hands to form a ball of dough. This will be quite sticky.

Tip the dough out onto a well-floured surface and knead for about 5 minutes until smooth. Place in a lightly oiled bowl and cover with cling film or a clean teacloth. Leave somewhere warm for an hour to prove or until the dough has doubled in size.

Once risen, knock (punch) back the dough then shape it into a round loaf. Place it on the baking tray and cover with a clean tea towel. Leave to rise somewhere warm for a further 45–60 minutes or doubled in size. Heat the oven to 220°C and bake for 25–30 minutes or until the base sounds hollow when tapped. Transfer to a wire rack to cool completely. The bread will keep fresh for a day or two and can be toasted thereafter.

MALTED WHOLEGRAIN LOAF

Makes 1 loaf

Prep time: 20 minutes + 45–60 minutes rising time + 45 minutes proving time

Cooking time: 30 minutes

This easy recipe is for a standard loaf made from a mix of malted wholegrain flour and strong white bread flour. The malted flour introduces a lovely nutty texture as well as a mellow flavour to the bread.

INGREDIENTS

300g strong white bread flour

200g malted wholegrain flour

1 x 7g packet of easy bake dried yeast

1½ teaspoons salt

1 teaspoon dark muscovado or dark brown sugar

325ml warm water

1 tablespoon olive oil + extra for greasing

METHOD

Lightly grease and sprinkle a little flour onto a 23 x 13cm loaf tin and set aside.

Combine the two types of flour, yeast and salt in a mixing bowl.

Dissolve the sugar in the warm water in a jug then stir this and the oil into the flour mixture. Then bring everything together with your hands to form a soft ball of dough.

Turn the dough out onto a floured board and knead it for 8–10 minutes or until it is smooth and elastic, and not sticky.

Lightly oil your bowl and put in the dough. Cover with a clean tea towel or cling film and leave somewhere warm for 45–60 minutes or until the dough has doubled in size.

Knock (punch) back the dough, shape it into a loaf then transfer to the loaf tin, cover and leave to prove in the same warm place for a further 45 minutes.

With 15 or so minutes of proving time to go, heat the oven to 220°C and place a loaf tin in the bottom of the oven. Once you have put the bread dough in the oven, carefully half fill the hot loaf tin with cold water. This will create steam in the oven and give your bread a good crust. Bake for around 30 minutes or until the base of the bread sounds hollow when tapped. Remove the bread from the oven, then transfer to a wire rack to cool completely. The bread will keep for 2–3 days in a bread container.

OATCAKES WITH SUNFLOWER SEEDS

Makes around 12 oatcakes

Prep time: 15 minutes

Cooking time: 30 minutes

Oatcakes are the classic Scottish flat savoury biscuit made from oatmeal, oats, fat, salt and water and are very easy to make. Traditionally, they would have been cooked on a griddle or girdle over an open fire. Often served with cheese, these go well with a vegan cheddar or cream cheese and with a little beetroot or chutney on the top.

INGREDIENTS

250g medium oatmeal

50g porridge oats

25g sunflower seeds

½ teaspoon bicarbonate of soda

½ teaspoon salt

50g cold vegan block butter (such as Naturli)

Around 75ml–100ml hot water

METHOD

Heat the oven to 200°C. Lightly flour a large baking tray.

Combine the oatmeal, oats, sunflower seeds, bicarbonate of soda and salt in a mixing bowl.

Add the vegan butter and cut it into the flour, then rub it between your fingertips until it resembles rough breadcrumbs. Add 75ml of the water and bring the mixture together with your hands to make a ball of dough. Add the remaining water a little at a time if needed. You are looking for quite a sticky dough.

Tip the dough onto a floured surface and roll it out to around ½ cm thick. Cut out the oatcakes with a biscuit cutter and re-roll and repeat until all the dough is used.

Put the oatcakes on the baking sheet and bake for 20 minutes. Then take the tray out of the oven, turn the oatcakes over and put them back in the oven to cook for a further 10 minutes or until golden brown. Remove from the oven and transfer to a wire rack to cool completely. These will keep for a week or more in an airtight container.

SEED CRACKERS

Makes around 30 crackers

Prep time: 10–15 minutes

Cooking time: 20 minutes

These three-seed crackers can be spread with any number of delicious toppings, such as vegan cream cheese, mushroom paté or hummus. The crackers are a healthy snack and contain iron and protein as well as calcium from the sesame seeds and Omega-3 fats from the flaxseeds.

INGREDIENTS

150g wholemeal flour or wholemeal spelt flour

25g flaxseeds

25g pumpkin seeds

25g sesame seeds

½ teaspoon salt

A few grinds of black pepper

1 tablespoon of olive oil or rapeseed oil

Cold water to mix

METHOD

Line two baking trays with greaseproof baking paper.

Place the flour, flaxseeds, pumpkin seeds, sesame seeds, and the salt and pepper into a bowl and stir well to combine.

Add the oil and enough water to bring the mixture together to form a ball of dough. The dough should be soft and pliable, neither sticky nor dry and crumbly. If you overdo the water, you can add a little more flour. If the dough is too crumbly, add a little more water – a very little at a time.

Place the dough between two sheets of greaseproof baking paper on a board and roll it out to around 3mm. Remove the top sheet of baking paper and cut out your crackers with a biscuit cutter. Re-roll and cut out further crackers until you have used all the dough.

Transfer to the baking sheet and chill for 30 minutes. Heat the oven to 190°C and bake the crackers for 20 minutes or until golden brown. Transfer to a wire rack to cool completely before serving. They will keep in an airtight container for at least a week.

SELKIRK BANNOCK

Makes 1 loaf

Prep time: 15–20 minutes + 60 minutes rising time + 45 minutes proving time

Cooking time: around 25 minutes

This famous sweet bannock hails from a bakery in Selkirk's market square in the Scottish Borders. According to Janet Warren's *A Feast of Scotland*, it was a teatime favourite of Queen Victoria when she was visiting nearby Abbotsford. Traditional recipes are very rich, using butter, lard, milk, sugar, currants, sultanas and mixed peel. My vegan version reduces the amount of sugar and fat while retaining the flavour and texture of the original.

INGREDIENTS

275g strong white bread flour + extra for dusting

150ml soya milk + extra for glazing

30g soft brown sugar

40g vegan butter (block butter is best, such as Naturli)

1 x 7g sachet easy bake dried yeast

A pinch of salt

100g sultanas

30g candied mixed peel

METHOD

Line a baking tray with greaseproof baking paper and dust with flour. Heat the soya milk and sugar in a saucepan on low heat until the sugar has dissolved. Set aside.

Put the flour in a mixing bowl. Cut in the vegan butter with a knife and then rub it between your fingertips until you have a mixture resembling breadcrumbs. Stir in the yeast and salt. Then add the milk mixture and bring everything together with a spoon and then with your hands to form a soft dough.

Knead the dough on a floured surface for 4–5 minutes until smooth and elastic. Lightly oil your mixing bowl and place the dough in it, cover with a clean tea towel or cling film, and place somewhere warm to rise for 60 minutes or until doubled in size.

Knock (punch) back the dough, then roll in the sultanas and candied peel and shape it into a rounded dome. Return the dough to the mixing bowl, cover, and allow it to rise again in a warm place for a further 45 minutes or until doubled in size.

Heat the oven to 190°C.

Once ready, transfer the dough to the baking tray and glaze the top with a little soya milk. Bake for 12 minutes then cover with silver foil to stop the fruit from burning and bake for a further 12–14 minutes or until risen and golden, and it sounds hollow when removed from the oven and tapped on the base. Transfer to a wire rack to cool completely. This will keep for a couple of days stored in a cool, dry place.

SPICED FRUIT LOAF

{Prepare in advance}

Makes 1 loaf

Prep time: 20–25 minutes

Cooking time: 60 minutes

This unleavened fruit loaf is full of dried fruit and spices as well as thick black treacle, and makes a lovely winter teatime accompaniment to a hot pot of tea. Prepare the loaf a few days before it is needed to allow the sticky treacle to work its magic and develop the loaf's full flavour. Serve with vegan butter for a really decadent treat.

INGREDIENTS

100ml hot-brewed Earl Grey or other lightly fragranced tea

100g sultanas

100g soft dates or prunes, chopped roughly

100ml black treacle

50g dark muscovado or dark brown sugar

50ml olive oil

Zest of 1 orange

250g wholemeal plain flour

1½ teaspoons baking powder

2 teaspoons ground ginger

1 teaspoon ground cinnamon

¼ teaspoon ground allspice

A pinch of salt

2 ripe bananas, peeled and mashed

METHOD

Heat the oven to 160°C. Line a small (roughly 20cm x 11cm) loaf tin with greaseproof baking paper.

Place the sultanas and dates or prunes into a bowl, pour the tea over and set aside.

Put the treacle, sugar, olive oil and orange zest in a pan on low heat and stir until the sugar has dissolved. Set aside.

Combine the flour, baking powder, ground ginger, cinnamon, allspice and salt in a mixing bowl. Next, add in the soaked fruit and tea, the sugar mixture and the mashed bananas and stir together well.

Pour into the prepared tin and bake for 60 minutes or until a skewer inserted in the loaf comes out clean.

Remove from the oven, cool in the tin for 20 minutes, then turn out onto a wire rack, peel off the greaseproof baking paper, and cool completely. Once cool, wrap in kitchen foil and let the loaf settle for at least 24 hours before eating. This keeps for at least a week.

3

CAKES

CARROT CAKE

Makes 1 x 20cm cake

Prep time: 20 minutes

Cooking time: 50–60 minutes

This moist carrot cake uses traditional spices and heart-healthy walnuts. With vitamin C from the orange juice, calcium from the treacle, iron from the raisins and protein from the nuts we are talking about a healthier type of all-plant-based cake which is also truly scrumptious.

INGREDIENTS

250g wholemeal plain flour

1½ teaspoons baking powder

½ teaspoon bicarbonate of soda

1 teaspoon ground cinnamon

½ teaspoon ground nutmeg

½ teaspoon ground mixed spice

A pinch of salt

100g soft brown sugar

50ml black treacle

Zest and juice of 1 medium orange + extra to make 150ml orange juice

50ml sunflower oil or olive oil

½ teaspoon apple cider vinegar

200g carrots, trimmed and grated

80g walnuts, chopped quite finely

80g raisins

2 tablespoons plain or vanilla soya yoghurt

To decorate

1x recipe for Cream Cheese Frosting (see p. 27) or Cashew Vanilla Frosting (see p. 24)

20g pistachios, chopped roughly

METHOD

Preheat the oven to 180°C. Line a round 20cm baking tin with greaseproof baking paper.

Sift the flour, baking powder, bicarbonate of soda and spices into a bowl, then add the salt and sugar and mix well together.

Heat the treacle, orange juice, oil and apple cider vinegar over a low heat, stirring often. Add the treacle mixture to the flour mixture and stir to combine.

Then stir in the orange zest, grated carrots, chopped walnuts, raisins and yoghurt and mix well. Tip into the baking tin and smooth the top. Add a baking collar or belt to the tin to distribute the heat evenly. Then bake for 50–60 minutes or until a skewer inserted into the cake comes out with just a few crumbs.

While the cake is cooking you can make the frosting.

Once cooked, remove the cake from the oven, cool in the tin for 15 minutes, then turn it out onto a wire rack to cool completely.

To Assemble the Cake

With a spatula, cover the top of the cake with Cream Cheese Frosting or Cashew Vanilla Frosting and then sprinkle the chopped pistachios over the top. This cake will keep for 2–3 days in an airtight container.

A word about . . . carrots

Carrots are a great source of beta carotene, an antioxidant which your body converts into vitamin A, as well as fibre, vitamin K1 and potassium. Adding carrots to your bakes provides moisture as well as sweetness, which means you can add slightly less sugar to your cake mix.

CHOCOLATE, BEETROOT AND CARDAMOM CAKE

Makes 1 x 20cm cake

Prep time: 25–30 minutes

Cooking time: 50–60 minutes

This is a chocolate cake with a difference; spiced with cardamom and with Scottish beetroot playing a starring role. It's a moist, almost truffle-like chocolate cake, which is covered with a rich ganache topping. A celebration cake for special occasions.

INGREDIENTS

200g wholemeal plain flour

45g cocoa powder

1 teaspoon baking powder

1 teaspoon bicarbonate of soda

1½ teaspoons ground cardamom

A pinch of salt

250g cooked beetroot, chopped

150g vegan dark chocolate (at least 54% cocoa solids), broken into pieces

100ml sunflower oil

1 teaspoon apple cider vinegar

1 teaspoon vanilla extract

6 tablespoons plain, unsweetened soya yoghurt

150ml soya milk

150g dark muscovado or dark brown sugar

To decorate

1 x recipe for Chocolate Ganache (see p. 26)

METHOD

Heat the oven to 180°C. Lightly grease a 20cm round cake tin and cover the base with a circle of greaseproof baking paper.

Combine the flour, cocoa powder, baking powder, bicarbonate of soda, cardamom and salt in a mixing bowl. Set aside.

Blend the beetroot in a mini blender or blender attachment of a food processor until smooth. Set aside.

Melt the chocolate in a *bain marie* or in a heatproof bowl set over a saucepan of simmering water, making sure the bowl doesn't touch the water. Set aside.

Whisk together the oil, apple cider vinegar, vanilla extract, soya yoghurt and soya milk in a jug. Then stir the sugar into this mixture.

Then add the blended beetroot, melted chocolate and the oil and milk mixture to the flour mixture and stir together until well combined.

Tip the mixture into the cake tin and smooth the top. Add a baking collar or belt to the tin to distribute the heat evenly. Then bake for 50–60 minutes or until a skewer inserted into the cake comes out clean.

Once the cake is cooked, cool for 15 minutes in the tin, then turn it out onto a wire rack and remove the baking paper. Cool completely before adding the ganache. This will keep in an airtight container for 2–3 days.

A word about . . . beetroot

Beetroot contains a good quantity of folate (vitamin B9), essential for red blood cell formation and healthy metabolism, as well as boron, together with small amounts of iron, magnesium, manganese, potassium and zinc. Fresh beetroot also contains vitamin C and fibre.

COCONUT AND LEMON CAKE

Makes 1 x 2-layered 18cm cake

Prep time: 15 minutes

Cooking time: 25–30 minutes

This is a rich and very moreish celebration cake with its sharp notes of lemon offset by naturally sweet desiccated coconut and filled with lemon curd and coconut cream. It really allows coconut and lemon to shine.

You can use pineapple jam as an alternative filling if you don't want to make – or cannot get hold of – vegan lemon curd.

INGREDIENTS

300ml full-fat coconut milk (from a tin)

60ml sunflower oil

1 teaspoon vanilla extract

Zest of 1 lemon + 1½ tablespoons lemon juice

300g white self-raising flour

1 teaspoon baking powder

55g desiccated coconut + extra for decorating (optional)

125g caster sugar

A pinch of salt

To fill and decorate

225ml vegan lemon curd (see recipe for Lemon Curd on p. 31)

150ml coconut cream (from a 250ml carton), chilled (until firm)

Icing sugar

Coconut chips or extra desiccated coconut (optional)

METHOD

Heat the oven to 180°C. Lightly grease 2 x 18cm round cake tins and line the bases with a circle of greaseproof baking paper.

Mix together the coconut milk, oil, vanilla extract and lemon juice in a jug and set aside (the mixture will curdle which is what you want).

Combine the flour, baking powder, desiccated coconut, sugar, salt and lemon zest in a mixing bowl. Next, carefully stir the coconut milk mixture into the flour mixture until fully combined.

Weigh the batter evenly into the baking tins, add a baking collar or belt to each tin to distribute the heat evenly, then bake in the oven for 25–30 minutes until golden brown on top and a skewer inserted into the middle of the cakes comes out clean.

Remove the cakes from the oven and cool in the tins for 15 minutes before turning out onto a wire rack, peeling off the baking paper and cooling completely.

To Assemble the Cake

Sandwich the two cakes together with the vegan lemon curd and coconut cream and dust the top of the cake with icing sugar. For extra decoration, you can add coconut chips or desiccated coconut.

This will keep, covered and in a cool place, for 2–3 days.

COFFEE CAKE

Makes 1 x 2-layered 20cm cake

Prep time: 15 minutes

Cooking time: 25–30 minutes

This is a nostalgia cake for me – it reminds me of Sunday afternoon teatime as a child. It's utterly delicious. Use a good quality coffee – either your favourite freshly ground and brewed coffee or an instant espresso for that deep, rich coffee flavour.

INGREDIENTS

250ml soya milk

1 teaspoon apple cider vinegar

2 tablespoons instant espresso powder

2 tablespoons boiling water

300g white self-raising flour

1½ teaspoons baking powder

A pinch of salt

175g caster sugar

70ml sunflower oil

1 teaspoon vanilla extract

To fill and decorate

1 x recipe for Coffee Buttercream (see p. 27)

10 walnut halves

METHOD

Lightly grease 2 x 20cm round cake tins and line the bases with a circle of greaseproof baking paper.

Mix together the soya milk and apple cider vinegar in a jug and set aside to curdle and make vegan buttermilk.

Mix together the espresso powder and boiling water in a cup and set aside to cool.

Put the flour, baking powder, salt and sugar in a mixing bowl and combine.

Measure the sunflower oil and vanilla extract into the curdled soya milk mixture and combine. Then stir this into the flour mixture followed by the coffee mixture.

Weigh the mixture out between the cake tins and smooth the top. Add a baking collar or belt to the tin to distribute the heat evenly, then bake for 25–30 minutes. The sponges are done when a skewer inserted into the middle of each comes out clean.

Remove from the oven and leave in the tin for 15 minutes then turn both sponges out onto a wire rack, peel off the baking paper and cool completely.

To Assemble the Cake

Spread the bottom sponge with half of the Coffee Buttercream then sandwich together with the second sponge. Cover the second sponge with the remaining buttercream and decorate with the walnuts.

This cake will keep for 2–3 days in an airtight container left in a cool place.

CRANACHAN CHEESECAKE

Makes 1 x 20cm cheesecake

Base
1 x Cheesecake Base
(see recipes on p. 25)

Filling
Prep time: 15 minutes + chilling time

A quintessentially Scottish filling for a delicious afternoon tea treat. This cheesecake includes the typical cranachan ingredients – toasted oatmeal, raspberries, whisky and cream – together with vegan cream cheese, and elderflower cordial as a replacement for whisky, if preferred.

INGREDIENTS

75g medium oatmeal or pinhead oatmeal

220ml vegan whipping cream (such as Coconut Collaborative double cream)

100g vegan cream cheese (such as Violife)

300g fresh raspberries + extra for decorating

1 tablespoon whisky or 1½ teaspoons elderflower syrup

Maple syrup to taste

1 tablespoon coconut butter, melted and cooled

METHOD

Toast the oatmeal in a frying pan on low heat. Set aside to cool.

Whisk the cream in a bowl until it reaches dropping consistency. Then mix in the cream cheese until smooth. Fold in the raspberries and smush them so that the cream becomes pink. Stir in the oatmeal and whisky or elderflower syrup and mix well. Add maple syrup according to taste. Then stir in the coconut butter.

To Assemble the Cheesecake

Tip the filling into the base and smooth the top. Decorate with raspberries and cool in the fridge until ready to serve. This is best eaten the day it is made as the base will go soggy after a day or so.

DUNDEE CAKE

{Prepare in advance}

Makes 1 x 20cm cake

Prep time: 25–30 minutes + at least 8 hours' soaking time

Cooking time: around 1 hour 30 minutes

An absolute classic Scottish rich fruit cake thought to have been made for Mary Queen of Scots in the 16th century, although the recipe we know today was developed in Dundee in the early 18th century. The main ingredients are raisins, currants, orange peel, nutmeg, almonds and marmalade. This vegan version follows the traditional flavours as well as the distinctive circular pattern of blanched almonds on the top, although adds some dried apricots, dates and glacé cherries.

INGREDIENTS

125g raisins

125g sultanas

50g soft pitted dates, chopped roughly

50g dried apricots, chopped roughly

50g glacé cherries, chopped roughly

Zest of 1 orange

Juice of one orange + enough extra orange juice to make 125ml

2 tablespoons whisky or soya milk

3 tablespoons orange marmalade

1 tablespoon ground flax seeds

3 tablespoons cold water

75ml olive oil or sunflower oil

120g soft brown sugar

25g ground almonds

225g wholemeal plain flour

1½ teaspoons baking powder

1 teaspoon ground mixed spice

A pinch of salt

To decorate

50g whole blanched almonds

METHOD

Line a 20cm round spring-form baking tin with greaseproof baking paper.

Put the raisins, sultanas, dates, apricots, cherries, orange zest, orange juice, whisky or soya milk and marmalade in a large bowl, and mix together well. Cover and leave for at least 8 hours or overnight in a cool place.

Mix the ground flax seeds and water together in a cup and set aside to gel.

After steeping, stir the oil, flax egg and sugar into the fruit mixture. Then add the ground almonds, flour, baking powder, mixed spice and salt and combine well. The batter will be quite stiff. Tip the mixture into the baking tin and smooth the top.

Heat the oven to 160°C.

Place the blanched almonds on top of the cake mixture in concentric circles evenly spaced apart working from the outside edge into the middle.

Add a baking collar or belt to the tin to distribute the heat evenly, then bake for 1 hour 30 minutes (cover after 1 hour with kitchen foil if the top of the cake is catching) or until a skewer inserted into the cake comes out clean. Remove from the oven and cool in the tin for 30 minutes. Then turn out onto a wire rack, peel off the baking paper and cool completely. Wrap in kitchen foil. This will keep for several weeks.

GLAMIS CAKE

Makes 1 x 20cm cake

Prep time: 25 minutes

Cooking time: 40–45 minutes

This is my vegan version of a Glamis Cake, essentially a rich and sticky date and walnut cake. There is a village of Glamis in Angus, Scotland, as well as a castle from which this cake perhaps has its origins.

INGREDIENTS

200g pitted soft dates or pitted Medjool dates, chopped roughly

250g wholemeal plain flour

1½ teaspoons baking powder

½ teaspoon bicarbonate of soda

A pinch of salt

100ml date syrup

250ml soya milk or oat milk

30ml sunflower oil

½ teaspoon apple cider vinegar

1 teaspoon vanilla extract

60g walnuts, chopped roughly

METHOD

Line a 20cm x 20cm loaf tin with greaseproof baking paper.

Put the dates in a heatproof bowl and cover them with 300ml boiling water. Set aside to soak for 15 minutes and then drain off the water.

Combine the flour, baking powder, bicarbonate of soda and salt in a mixing bowl.

Heat the oven to 180°C.

Warm the date syrup, soya or oat milk and oil in a saucepan on low heat, stirring occasionally. Remove from the heat and stir in the apple cider vinegar and vanilla extract.

Pour the date syrup mixture into the flour mixture and stir until well combined. Then fold in the soaked chopped dates and the walnuts. Pour the batter into the prepared baking tin and smooth the top. Add a baking collar or belt to the tin to distribute the heat evenly, then bake for 40–45 minutes or until a skewer inserted into the middle of the cake comes out with just a little stickiness.

Remove from the oven, and cool completely in the tin before turning out onto a wire rack and peeling off the baking paper. Once cool, wrap in clean greaseproof baking paper or foil and place in an airtight container until needed. This cake keeps for up to a week.

A word about . . . walnuts

Walnuts are rich in vitamin E and fibre, and contain more of the good Omega-3 fats than any other widely available nut. They are also full of antioxidants.

LEMON AND POPPY SEED CAKE

Makes 1 loaf

Prep time: 15–20 minutes

Cooking time: 35–40 minutes

This lemony cake is full of lemon zest and juice, and delicious just as it is with a dusting of icing sugar on top. However, you can also cover it with Lemon Icing (see recipe on p. 32) if you fancy a sweet and citrusy topping.

INGREDIENTS

225g white self-raising flour

50g ground almonds

1 teaspoon baking powder

A pinch of salt

145g caster sugar

1 tablespoon poppy seeds

Zest of 2 lemons and juice of 1½ lemons

50ml sunflower oil

180ml soya milk

1 teaspoon vanilla extract

METHOD

Heat the oven to 180°C. Lightly grease and line a 23cm x 13cm loaf tin with greaseproof baking paper.

Stir together the flour, almonds, baking powder, salt, sugar, poppy seeds and lemon zest in a mixing bowl. Combine the sunflower oil, soya milk, lemon juice and vanilla extract in a jug (it will curdle and form vegan buttermilk), then gently stir this into the flour mixture.

Tip the batter into the loaf tin, and level the top. Add a baking collar or belt to the tin to distribute the heat evenly, then bake for 35–40 minutes or until the cake has risen and is golden brown, and a skewer inserted into the cake comes out clean.

Remove from the oven and cool for 15 minutes, then turn the cake out onto a wire rack, take off the baking paper and cool completely. Cover with lemon icing or a dusting of icing sugar before serving. The cake will keep for 2–3 days in an airtight container.

MARMALADE CAKE

Makes 1 x 18cm cake

Prep time: 15 minutes

Cooking time: 45 minutes

This is a quick and easy teatime cake to make, full of the bitter-sweet flavour of marmalade. It is quite a sticky cake, and a real favourite. Use a good-quality marmalade – ideally from Dundee!

INGREDIENTS

275ml unsweetened soya milk

1 teaspoon apple cider vinegar

250g wholemeal self-raising flour (or 250g wholemeal plain flour + 1½ teaspoons baking powder)

115g soft brown sugar

A pinch of salt

60ml olive oil or sunflower oil

3 tablespoons orange marmalade

To decorate

1 x recipe for Marmalade Glaze (see recipe on p. 32)

METHOD

Heat the oven to 180°C. Lightly grease and line an 18cm round baking tin with greaseproof baking paper.

Combine the soya milk and apple cider vinegar in a bowl and set aside to curdle and form vegan buttermilk.

Sift the flour into a mixing bowl, then stir in the sugar and salt. Add the vegan buttermilk and the oil to the flour mixture and mix gently before stirring in the marmalade.

Pour the batter into the prepared baking tin, add a baking collar or belt to the tin to distribute the heat evenly, then bake in the oven for 45 minutes or until a skewer inserted into the cake comes out clean.

Once cooked, remove from the oven, leave in the tin for 15 minutes, then turn out onto a wire rack, take off the baking paper and cool completely. Then spread with the Marmalade Glaze. The cake will keep for 2–3 days in an airtight container.

PEAR AND GINGER CAKE

Makes 1 x 20cm cake

Prep time: 20 minutes

Cooking time: 45–55 minutes

Adding pears to a cake adds moisture and natural sweetness, and in this recipe the pears marry beautifully with the ginger. Adding stem ginger gives the cake an extra-special flavour and I recommend doing this. You could also try this recipe using pieces of chopped apple instead of pears.

INGREDIENTS

175ml soya milk

1 teaspoon apple cider vinegar

250g plain wholemeal flour

1½ teaspoons baking powder

½ teaspoon bicarbonate of soda

1½ teaspoons ground ginger

100g light soft brown sugar

A pinch of salt

60ml sunflower oil + extra for greasing

2 tablespoons apple sauce

2 pears, cored and cut into small pieces

1 piece of stem ginger in syrup, chopped finely (optional)

To decorate

A little icing sugar

or

1 x recipe for Gingerbread Buttercream (see p. 28)

METHOD

Heat the oven to 180°C. Lightly grease and line a 20cm round spring-form cake tin with baking parchment.

Mix the soya milk with the apple cider vinegar and set aside to form vegan buttermilk.

Combine the flour, baking powder, bicarbonate of soda, ground ginger, sugar and salt in a mixing bowl.

Add the sunflower oil to the soya milk mixture and then stir it into the flour mixture together with the apple sauce and combine well. Then fold in the pears and the stem ginger, if using.

Tip the mixture into the baking tin, add a baking collar or belt to the tin to distribute the heat evenly, then bake for 45–55 minutes or until a skewer inserted into the cake comes out clean.

Remove the cake from the oven and cool in the tin for 15 minutes. Then turn out onto a wire rack, remove the baking paper and cool completely. Once cool, dust with a little icing sugar, or alternatively the Gingerbread Buttercream works well spread on top. Serve with vegan cream, if liked.

This will keep for 1–2 days covered and stored in a cool place.

A word about . . . pears

Pears are a rich source of folate, vitamin C, copper and potassium as well as fibre and antioxidants. Pears are lovely chopped onto muesli or porridge, or added to salads.

PISTACHIO AND LEMON SQUARE CAKE

Makes 1 x 20cm square cake

Prep time: 15 minutes

Cooking time 35–40 minutes

This is a real treat for any time of day, which I make in a square tin, hence the name 'square' cake. The wholemeal flour adds some fibre while the lemon offers some vitamin C; and the nuts and soya milk add protein. This is still a cake rather than a health food – a sweet, nutty one.

INGREDIENTS

250ml unsweetened soya milk

1 teaspoon apple cider vinegar

250g wholemeal flour

1½ teaspoons baking powder

A pinch of salt

125g soft brown sugar

65g shelled pistachios, ground roughly (reserve 15g for decorating)

Zest of 1 lemon + 2 teaspoons freshly squeezed lemon juice

60ml sunflower oil

2 tablespoons apple sauce

To decorate

1x recipe for Lemon Icing (see recipe on p. 32)

The remaining pistachios

METHOD

Heat the oven to 180°C. Lightly grease and line a 20cm square cake tin with greaseproof baking paper.

Mix the soya milk and apple cider vinegar in a jug and set aside to form vegan buttermilk.

Combine the flour, baking powder, salt, sugar, 50g of the ground pistachios and the lemon zest in a mixing bowl.

Stir the oil and lemon juice into the soya milk mixture then add this to the flour mixture and combine. Fold in the apple sauce.

Tip the batter into the baking tin, add a baking collar or belt to the tin to distribute the heat evenly, then bake for 35–40 minutes or until a skewer comes out clean when inserted into the middle of the cake.

Remove from the oven and cool the cake in the tin for 15 minutes before transferring to a wire rack and removing the greaseproof baking paper. Cool completely before drizzling over the Lemon Icing and decorating with the remaining ground pistachios. The cake will keep for 2–3 days in a cake tin.

A word about . . . pistachios

Pistachios are rich in antioxidants, healthy fats, fibre and protein. They contain vitamin B6 and thiamine as well as calcium, copper, iron, magnesium and manganese.

RASPBERRY FRANGIPANE CAKE

Makes 1 x 20cm cake

Prep time: 15–20 minutes

Cooking time: 40–45 minutes

I love almond-flavoured cakes and this frangipane is a classic – probably French or Italian in origin, but made quintessentially Scottish by the addition of fresh raspberries, ideally from Angus, Perthshire or Fife!

INGREDIENTS

200ml soya milk

1 teaspoon apple cider vinegar

250g wholemeal flour + extra for coating the raspberries

1½ teaspoons baking powder

A pinch of salt

50g ground almonds

125g caster sugar

60ml sunflower oil

1½ teaspoons almond extract

100g fresh (Scottish) raspberries

2 tablespoons high fruit content raspberry conserve

To decorate

30g flaked almonds

METHOD

Heat the oven to 180°C. Lightly grease the base and sides of a 20cm round springform baking tin and line with greaseproof baking paper.

Mix the soya milk and apple cider vinegar in a jug and set aside to curdle and form vegan buttermilk.

Put the flour, baking powder, salt, ground almonds and caster sugar into a mixing bowl and stir together.

Stir the oil and the almond extract into the vegan buttermilk.

Sprinkle a little flour onto a plate and then roll the raspberries in the flour to lightly coat them (this will help prevent them from sinking as the cake cooks).

Tip the buttermilk mixture into the flour mixture and combine. Then stir in the raspberry conserve and fold in the raspberries. Don't worry if the raspberries begin to break up, just incorporate them into the batter.

Tip the mixture into the baking tin and even it out. Sprinkle the flaked almonds over the top. Add a baking collar or belt to the tin to distribute the heat evenly, then bake for 40–45 minutes or until the top has browned and a skewer inserted into the middle of the cake comes out clean.

Once cooked, remove from the oven and allow to cool in the tin for 15 minutes before turning out onto a wire rack and removing the baking paper. Cool completely before placing on a cake plate and covering.

Serve with fresh raspberries and cream if liked! The cake will keep for 3–4 days, covered, in a cool place.

Tip: I encourage you to use wholemeal plain flour in this recipe rather than white plain flour. If you use white flour the raspberry conserve may turn the cake a pale grey colour!

STICKY GINGERBREAD

{Prepare in advance}

Makes 1 loaf

Prep time: 20 minutes

Cooking time: 45–50 minutes

There are many recipes for Scottish gingerbread. Traditionally, Edinburgh gingerbread includes almonds and eggs, while gingerbread from the town of Fochabers in Speyside includes fruit, spices and almonds as well as an unusual ingredient: beer! This vegan version is a nod towards Fochabers. It is a spiced gingery delight whether for elevenses or teatime.

INGREDIENTS

1 tablespoon ground flax seeds

3 tablespoons water

250g wholemeal plain flour

1 teaspoon baking powder

1 teaspoon bicarbonate of soda

50g dark muscovado or dark brown sugar

2 teaspoons ground ginger

1 teaspoon cinnamon

1 teaspoon ground mixed spice

A pinch of salt

60g soft vegan butter (such as Vitalite)

100g black treacle

175ml vegan beer or stout (such as Dark Island Dark Ale)

75g sultanas

2 pieces of stem ginger, chopped finely

METHOD

Heat the oven to 180°C. Line a 23cm x 13cm loaf tin with greaseproof baking paper.

Mix the ground flax seeds with the water and set aside to gel.

Combine the flour, baking powder, bicarbonate of soda, sugar, ground ginger, cinnamon, mixed spice and salt in a mixing bowl.

Melt the butter and treacle on low heat in a saucepan. Add this mixture to the flour mixture together with the flax seed mixture and the vegan beer or stout and mix gently. Then mix in the sultanas and stem ginger.

Tip the batter into the baking tin and smooth the top. Add a baking collar or belt to the tin to distribute the heat evenly, then bake for around 45–50 minutes or until a skewer inserted into the middle of the cake comes out clean.

Remove from the oven and allow to cool completely in the tin. Once cooled, double wrap the gingerbread in greaseproof baking paper or kitchen foil and leave for at least 24 hours before eating to allow the full flavour of the cake to develop. It will keep, wrapped and left in a cool place, for at least a week.

VICTORIA SPONGE

{Prepare the jam and cream in advance}

Makes 1 x 2-layered 18cm sponge cake

Prep time: 15 minutes

Cooking time: 25–30 minutes

A Victoria sponge is an all-time favourite that can be enjoyed any time – even as a birthday cake! This vegan version uses vegan buttermilk and self-raising flour instead of eggs. The real secret to making a successful vegan sponge that has a good rise is to melt and cool the vegan butter.

INGREDIENTS

150g soft vegan butter (such as Vitalite) + extra for greasing

275ml soya milk

1 teaspoon apple cider vinegar

300g white self-raising flour

½ teaspoon bicarbonate of soda

150g caster sugar

A pinch of salt

1 teaspoon vanilla extract

To fill

Strawberry and Elderflower Chia Jam (see recipe on p. 37) or a high fruit content strawberry jam

Whipped Cream (see recipe on p. 40) or a shop bought vegan whipping cream

Icing sugar to dust

METHOD

Heat the oven to 180°C. Lightly grease the base and sides of 2 x 18cm round sandwich tins and line the bases with greaseproof baking paper.

Put the vegan butter in a small pan on low heat and let it melt. Then set aside to cool.

Mix the soya milk and apple cider vinegar in a bowl to make vegan buttermilk.

Mix the flour, bicarbonate of soda, sugar and salt together in a bowl. Then add the melted butter, buttermilk and vanilla extract and stir together gently. Do not overmix.

Weigh the batter evenly between the two baking tins and smooth the top with a palette knife. Add a baking collar or belt to the tin to distribute the heat evenly, then bake for 25–30 minutes until light golden brown on top or until a skewer inserted in the middle of each sponge cake comes out clean.

Remove the cakes from the oven and cool for 10 minutes in the tins before turning out onto a wire rack to cool completely and removing the baking parchment paper.

To Assemble the Cake

Once completely cool, cover one of the layers of sponge cake with a generous amount of jam, followed by a thick layer of cream. Place the second layer of sponge cake on top of the bottom sponge and sandwich the two together. Transfer to a plate and dust a little icing sugar over the top.

This cake is best eaten the day it is made, although it will keep for another day or two covered and placed somewhere cool and dry.

4

SCONES

AYRSHIRE SCONES

Makes 6–8 small scones

Prep time: 15 minutes

Cooking time: 10–12 minutes

A NOTE ON SCONES

The *Scottish National Dictionary* defines a scone as 'A large round cake of wheat or barley flour baked on an iron plate or GIRDLE and generally cut across into three-cornered pieces also called *scones*'. Modern-day scones are baked in the oven and can be round or triangular. I have provided a number of different recipes here reflecting scone-making from different areas of Scotland.

AYRSHIRE SCONES

As with shortbread, in Ayrshire on the west coast of Scotland they make their scones with cream, which makes them very rich. I substitute oat cream for dairy cream here, although you could use soya or any other plant-based cream.

INGREDIENTS

55ml oat milk or soya milk + extra for glazing

1 teaspoon lemon juice

225g white self-raising flour + extra for rolling out the dough

1 teaspoon baking powder

A pinch of salt

25g caster sugar

40g vegan butter (block butter is best, such as Naturli)

45ml oat cream or soya cream

METHOD

Heat the oven to 220°C and line a baking tray with greaseproof baking paper.

Combine the oat milk or the soya milk and lemon juice in a bowl to make vegan buttermilk. Set aside.

Stir together the flour, baking powder, salt and sugar in a mixing bowl. Cut the vegan butter into the flour and rub it in with your fingertips until the mixture resembles breadcrumbs. Next, stir in the milk mixture and cream and bring the mixture together to form a soft dough.

Sprinkle flour onto a clean surface and roll out the dough until it is around 3cm thick. Cut out the scones with a 7cm biscuit cutter re-rolling any remnants and cutting out until all the dough has been used – and place them on the baking sheet. Dab the top of each with a little vegan milk.

Place in the preheated oven and cook for 10–12 minutes. Remove from the oven, transfer to a wire rack and serve warm with Strawberry and Elderflower Chia Jam (see p. 37) and Whipped Cream (see p. 40) or with Lemon Curd (see p. 31). The scones are best eaten the day they are made, and are delicious when warm, although they can be stored in an airtight container and reheated or eaten when cool.

'CHEESE' AND CAYENNE PEPPER SCONES

Makes 6–8 small scones

Prep time: 15 minutes

Cooking time: 12–14 minutes

Scones are versatile and can be sweet or savoury. I love a savoury scone, warm from the oven, spread with a little vegan butter. These scones have a hint of heat from the cayenne pepper and the combination of vegan cheese, nutritional yeast and mustard provide a distinctive 'cheese' flavour.

INGREDIENTS

100ml soya milk + extra for glazing

1 teaspoon apple cider vinegar

½ teaspoon English mustard

125g white self-raising flour + extra for rolling out the dough

125g spelt wholemeal flour

1½ teaspoons baking powder

¼ teaspoon cayenne pepper

A pinch of salt

40g vegan butter (block butter is best, such as Naturli)

40g vegan cheese, grated (such as Violife Epic or similar cheddar-style cheese)

METHOD

Heat the oven to 220°C and line a baking tray with greaseproof baking paper.

Combine the soya milk and apple cider vinegar in a bowl to make vegan buttermilk. Then mix in the mustard. Set aside.

Stir together the flour, baking powder, cayenne pepper and salt in a mixing bowl. Cut the butter into the flour mixture and then rub it between your fingertips into the flour until it resembles breadcrumbs. Then stir in the vegan cheese.

Add the milk mixture and bring everything together with your hands to form a dough.

On a lightly floured surface and with a floured rolling pin, roll out the dough until it is around 3cm thick. Cut out the scones with a 7cm biscuit cutter – re-rolling any remnants and cutting out until all the dough has been used – and place them on the baking sheet. Dab the tops with a little plant milk.

Place the scones on the prepared baking sheet and bake for 12–14 minutes. Remove from the oven, transfer to a wire rack and serve warm with vegan butter. The scones are best eaten the day they are made, and are delicious when warm, although they can be stored in an airtight container and reheated or eaten when cool.

DROP SCONES

Makes about 12 drop scones

Prep time: 5 minutes + 10 minutes resting time

Cooking time: about 5–6 minutes per batch

Drop scones are also known as 'Scotch pancakes' and they resemble a pancake more than a scone. These are easy to make and can be made sweet or savoury. For a savoury drop scone, just leave out the sugar from the recipe below. They can be eaten with a wide variety of toppings – such as fruit compote and yoghurt, jam, marmalade or maple syrup or, if you prefer them savoury, with cream cheese or peanut butter – and enjoyed at any time.

INGREDIENTS

110ml soya milk

1 teaspoon apple cider vinegar

110g plain white flour

½ teaspoon bicarbonate of soda

25g caster sugar

A pinch of salt

25ml sunflower oil or melted vegan butter

METHOD

Combine the soya milk and apple cider vinegar in a bowl and set aside to curdle and form vegan buttermilk.

Stir together the flour, bicarbonate of soda, sugar and salt in a bowl. Add the buttermilk and the oil or melted butter if using and mix well until smooth. Set aside for at least 10 minutes to let the batter settle. Don't skip this stage.

Heat a frying pan with a little oil on medium-high heat. Then drop as many tablespoons of the batter into the pan as will fit (you can use a round biscuit cutter as a mould for shaping if you like) and cook until golden and bubbles appear on the top. Flip the drop scones over and cook them on the other side. Serve warm or cold with your favourite toppings.

I use the savoury version as a base for my Carrot Lox (see recipe on p. 171).

FRUIT SCONES

Makes 6–8 small scones

Prep time: 15 minutes

Cooking time: 12 minutes

These are little baking gems, made with sultanas. If you prefer your scones entirely plain, just leave out the fruit. I prefer to make a small batch of scones as they are best fresh from the oven. If you have guests or want a larger quantity, just double the recipe.

INGREDIENTS

100ml soya milk or oat milk + extra for glazing

1 teaspoon apple cider vinegar

225g white self-raising flour + extra for rolling out the dough

1 teaspoon baking powder

25g caster sugar

A pinch of salt

40g vegan butter (block butter is best, such as Naturli)

40g sultanas

METHOD

Heat the oven to 220°C. Line a baking tray with greaseproof baking paper.

Combine the soya milk or oat milk and apple cider vinegar in a bowl and set aside for a couple of minutes to curdle and form vegan buttermilk.

Stir together the flour, baking powder, sugar and salt in a mixing bowl. Cut the butter into the flour mixture and then rub it into the flour until it resembles breadcrumbs. Stir in the sultanas. Then add the milk mixture and with your hands bring everything together to form a soft dough.

On a lightly floured surface and with a floured rolling pin, roll out the dough until it is around 3cm thick. Cut out the scones – re-rolling any remnants and cutting out until all the dough has been used – and place them on the baking sheet. Dab the tops with a little plant milk.

Place the scones on the prepared baking sheet and bake for 12 minutes. Remove from the oven, transfer to a wire rack and serve warm with vegan butter. The scones are best eaten the day they are made although they can be stored in an airtight container and reheated or eaten when cool.

Variations

Apricot Scones
Follow the recipe for Fruit Scones above but replace the sultanas with 40g chopped dried apricots.

Cherry Scones
Follow the recipe for Fruit Scones above but replace the sultanas with 40g chopped glacé cherries.

OATMEAL SCONE ROUND

Makes 4 triangular scones

Prep time: 15 minutes

Cooking time: 20–25 minutes

This is a traditional single large flat round scone made from oatmeal that is cut into triangles which would have been cooked on a griddle or girdle but which I bake in the oven. The scones make a great base for savoury toppings such as vegan cream cheese and Carrot Lox (see recipe on p. 171) or sweet toppings such as marmalade or Strawberry and Elderflower Chia Jam (see recipe on p. 37).

INGREDIENTS

100ml soya milk or oat milk + extra milk for glazing

1 teaspoon apple cider vinegar

195g white or wholemeal self-raising flour + extra for dusting

75g pinhead oatmeal or fine oatmeal

A tablespoon of soft brown sugar

½ teaspoon salt

40g vegan butter (block butter is best, such as Naturli)

METHOD

Heat the oven to 220°C. Line a baking tray with greaseproof baking paper.

Combine the soya milk or oat milk and apple cider vinegar in a bowl and set aside for a couple of minutes to curdle and form vegan buttermilk.

Stir together the flour, oatmeal, sugar and salt in a mixing bowl. Cut the butter into the flour mixture and then rub it into the flour until it resembles breadcrumbs. Then add the milk mixture and with your hands bring everything together to form a soft dough.

Press or roll out the dough on a floured surface into a circle, around 16cm in diameter and around 2cm thick. Score into 4 triangles and dab the top with soya milk. Place on the baking tray and bake for 18–20 minutes on the top and around 5 minutes on the other side or until golden brown. Transfer to a wire rack to cool before breaking into four pieces. Best eaten while warm on the day they are made, although they can be stored in an airtight container and reheated or eaten when cool.

SCONE RING

Makes 8 scones

Prep time: 20 minutes

Cooking time: 35–40 minutes

A Scottish scone ring is like a 'tear and share' bread for pulling apart when baked. It is round in shape but divided into triangles. A scone ring also traditionally includes sultanas, although you can substitute raisins, dates or cherries in like-for-like quantities if you prefer.

INGREDIENTS

150ml oat milk or soya milk + extra for glazing

1 teaspoon apple cider vinegar

375g white self-raising flour + extra for rolling

1½ teaspoons baking powder

A pinch of salt

60g vegan butter (block butter is best, such as Naturli)

60g caster sugar

60g sultanas

METHOD

Preheat the oven to 220°C. Line a baking tray with greaseproof baking paper.

Combine the oat milk or soya milk and apple cider vinegar in a bowl and set aside for a couple of minutes to curdle and form vegan buttermilk.

Stir together the flour, baking powder and salt in a mixing bowl. Cut the butter into the flour mixture and then rub it into the flour until it resembles breadcrumbs. Next, stir in the sugar and sultanas. Then add the milk mixture and with your hands bring everything together to form a soft dough.

Turn out the dough onto a floured worktop and knead it for a few minutes, then roll it into a circle of 18–20cm diameter and place it on the baking sheet. Dab the top all over with milk. Without cutting all the way through, score the dough into 8 even triangles.

Bake for 35–40 minutes or until risen and golden brown. Remove from the oven, transfer to a wire rack and serve warm with vegan butter and strawberry jam or with Strawberry and Elderflower Chia Jam (see recipe on p. 37) and Whipped Cream (see recipe on p. 40). The scones are best eaten the day they are made although they can be kept in an airtight container and reheated over the next day or two or eaten when cool.

TREACLE SCONES

Makes 6–8 scones

Prep time: 15 minutes

Cooking time: 12–14 minutes

Treacle scones are sweetened with black treacle, which as well as being sweet contains lots of healthy vitamins and minerals. They also contain ground mixed spice and ground ginger. They have a deeper flavour than a plain or fruit scone, and are darker in colour, though just as delicious.

INGREDIENTS

100ml soya milk or oat milk + extra for glazing

1 teaspoon lemon juice

250g wholemeal plain flour or wholemeal spelt flour

3 teaspoons baking powder

1 teaspoon ground ginger

½ teaspoon ground mixed spice

A pinch of salt

20g dark muscovado sugar

40g vegan butter (block butter is best, such as Naturli)

2 tablespoons black treacle

METHOD

Preheat the oven to 220°C. Line a baking sheet with greaseproof baking paper.

Combine the soya milk or oat milk and lemon juice and set aside for a couple of minutes to curdle and form vegan buttermilk.

Stir together the flour, baking powder, ginger, mixed spice, salt and sugar in a mixing bowl. Cut the butter into the flour mixture and then rub it between your fingertips into the flour until it resembles breadcrumbs.

Warm the treacle in a pan on low heat. Add the treacle and the milk mixture to the flour mixture and bring everything together with your hands to form a dough.

On a lightly floured surface and with a floured rolling pin, roll out the dough until it is around 3cm thick. Cut out the scones – re-rolling any remnants and cutting out until all the dough has been used – and place them on the baking sheet. Dab the tops with a little plant milk. Place the scones on the prepared baking sheet and bake for 12–14 minutes. Remove from the oven, transfer to a wire rack and serve warm.

The scones are best eaten the day they are made although they can be stored in an airtight container and reheated or eaten when cool.

5

TARTS

APPLE PECAN CRUMBLE TART

{The pastry, crumble topping and apples can all be prepared in advance}

Makes 1 x 20cm tart

Prep time: 20 minutes for the filling

Cooking time: 20 minutes (pastry) + 35–40 minutes (tart)

This apple tart has a pastry base, apple and cinnamon filling, and a pecan crumble topping and makes a lovely autumn afternoon treat.

You can also use the pecan crumble topping to make a fruit crumble for dessert with apples, pears or plums.

INGREDIENTS

Tart case and topping

1 x quantity Pecan Crumble Topping (see recipe on p. 33)

½ quantity Sweet Shortcrust Pastry (see recipe on p. 39).

Apple filling

3 large cooking apples (such as Bramley)

1 teaspoon ground cinnamon

1 tablespoon plain flour

2 tablespoons soft brown sugar

1 tablespoon vegan butter + extra for greasing

METHOD

Heat the oven to 180°C. Lightly grease a 20cm heatproof pie dish.

Roll out your pastry into a circle around 3mm thick and about 2cm larger than the pie dish you are using. Lay the pastry in the dish and up the sides, crimping the edges. Prick the base with a fork, then cover with greaseproof baking paper and baking beans (or dry rice) and part-bake ('blind') for 20 minutes. Take out of the oven and remove the baking beans (or rice if using) and baking paper. Set aside to cool.

Raise the oven temperature to 200°C. Peel then cut the apples into quarters, core them and cut them into slices and then chunks.

Tip: if you are preparing the apples in advance, place the cut apples in a bowl of cold water to which you have added several drops of lemon juice and weight down with a saucer. This will keep them from browning. Put the apples in the tart case, then sprinkle over the cinnamon, flour and sugar and dot with pieces of butter.

Then spoon over the Pecan Crumble Topping. You will have a high dome of topping over the apples and this will decrease as the apples and topping cook. Bake in the oven for 20 minutes then lower the temperature to 180°C and cook for a further 20 minutes. Cover with kitchen foil if the edges of the tart are overbaking. Remove from the oven and serve hot or warm with vegan custard, ice cream or cream.

A word about... apples

Apples are full of antioxidants. They also contain dietary fibre needed to support a healthy digestive system, as well as vitamins A and C that support the immune system, vitamin K needed for blood clotting, biotin (vitamin B7) that helps to break down fat, and iodine which is involved in healthy thyroid function.

BORDER TART

Makes 1 x 18cm tart

Prep time: 20–25 minutes for the filling

Cooking time: 20 minutes (pastry) + 15 minutes (tart)

Border tart is a rich fruit tart in sweet shortcrust pastry containing mixed dried fruit and an icing glaze, that hails from the Scottish Borders. It also goes by the name of Eyemouth tart.

Tip: when using creamed coconut, the coconut and the coconut fat may separate; make sure you use some of both when measuring out your quantities.

INGREDIENTS

Tart case

½ x quantity Sweet Shortcrust Pastry (see recipe on p. 39)

Filling

1 tablespoon ground flax seeds

3 tablespoons cold water

50g vegan butter

50g light brown sugar

50g creamed coconut (not coconut cream or coconut milk)

1 teaspoon vanilla extract

75g mixed dried fruit

30g glacé cherries, roughly chopped + extra for decorating

30g walnuts, roughly chopped

Zest of 1 lemon

To decorate

30g icing sugar

Fresh lemon juice as needed

METHOD

Heat the oven to 180°C.

Roll out the pastry on a floured surface to form a circle that will cover the base and sides of an 18cm fluted flan tin. Press the pastry into the tin/dish and prick the base all over with a fork. Cover the base with greaseproof baking paper and baking beans (or dry rice) and part-bake ('blind') for 15 minutes. Remove the baking beans (or rice if using) and baking paper and put the pastry back in the oven for a further 5 minutes, then remove from the oven and set aside while you make the filling.

Mix the ground flax seeds and water together in a cup and set aside to thicken into a flax egg.

Melt the vegan butter, sugar and creamed coconut in a saucepan. Take off the heat and whisk in the flax egg and vanilla extract. Add the mixed dried fruit, glacé cherries, walnuts and the lemon zest and mix well.

Tip the mixture into the pastry case and even it out, then bake for 15 minutes, covering with kitchen foil if the edges of the pastry are catching. The filling will be firm when cooked. Remove from the oven and cool completely before adding the icing.

To Decorate

Put the icing sugar in a bowl and add enough lemon juice to make a thick icing. Drizzle the icing in a lattice pattern over the tart.

The tart will keep for a week in an airtight container stored in a cool place.

CRANACHAN TARTS

Makes 12 tarts

Prep time: 10 minutes for the filling

Cooking time: 15 minutes

Cranachan is usually a dessert and is made from toasted oatmeal, raspberries, whisky and cream. For this recipe I have filled sweet pastry tart cases with a cranachan mixture. If you are making these for little ones or anyone who is teetotal, you could omit the whisky or replace it with elderflower cordial.

You can also use the no-bake Sweet Date and Nut Tart Case (see recipe on p. 38) to make these tarts.

INGREDIENTS

Tart cases

½ x recipe for Sweet Shortcrust Pastry (see p.39)

Filling

75g medium oatmeal or pinhead oatmeal

220ml vegan whipping cream (see recipe for Whipped Cream on p. 40) or a shop-bought vegan whipping cream (such as Coconut Collaborative double cream)

150g fresh raspberries

1 tablespoon whisky or 1½ teaspoons elderflower syrup

Maple syrup to taste

METHOD

Heat the oven to 180°C. Lightly grease a 12-hole baking tin.

Roll out the pastry on a floured surface to around 4mm thickness and cut out circles with a biscuit cutter a few centimetres larger than the holes in the tin. Put the pastry into the cases and press it into the base and sides. Bake for around 15 minutes then remove from the oven and leave to cool completely before removing from the tin.

While the pastry is baking you can make the filling.

Toast the oatmeal in a frying pan on low heat. Set aside to cool.

Whisk the cream in a bowl until it reaches dropping consistency. Then fold in the raspberries and smush them so that the cream becomes pink. Stir in the oatmeal and whisky or elderflower syrup and add maple syrup if needed according to taste.

To Assemble the Tarts

Divide the filling equally between the pastry cases and chill in the fridge until needed. These are best eaten the day they are made.

ECCLEFECHAN TART

Makes 1 tart

Prep time: 15 minutes for the filling

Cooking time: 15 minutes (pastry)
15 minutes (tart)

This delicious tart which is a combination of sticky toffee, raisins and crunchy nuts in a pastry case gets its name from the village of Ecclefechan in Dumfries and Galloway. The tart is often served as an alternative to mince pies at Christmas, and is rich and treacly.

INGREDIENTS

Tart case

½ quantity Sweet Shortcrust Pastry (see recipe on p. 39)

Filling

50g vegan butter

100g soft pitted dates, chopped roughly

2 tablespoons blackstrap molasses or black treacle

1 tablespoon date syrup

75g raisins

25g walnuts, chopped roughly

25g flaked almonds

1 teaspoon vanilla extract

Water as needed – about 2 tablespoons

METHOD

Heat the oven to 180°C. Set aside an 18cm round, fluted tart tin.

Roll out the pastry to 3mm thickness and about 3cm wider than the pie dish. Put the pastry in the dish and press it into the base and sides. Trim away any excess and discard. Prick the base with a fork, cover in greaseproof baking paper and fill with baking beans (or dry rice), then part-bake ('blind') for 15 minutes. Remove from the oven and set aside while you make the filling.

Melt the vegan butter in a saucepan. Add the dates, molasses or treacle and date syrup and cook on low heat, stirring continuously and mashing with a spoon until the dates have softened and you have a toffee-like consistency. Remove from the heat and stir in the raisins, walnuts, almonds and vanilla extract. Then add as much water as needed to loosen the mixture a little – about two tablespoons. Tip the mixture into the pastry base, distributing it evenly.

Bake for 15 minutes until the filling is firm to the touch. Remove from the oven and cool completely before serving. Cut into slices and serve with Almond Cream (see recipe on p. 21) or Whipped Cream (see recipe on p. 40).

FRUIT SLICES (FLY CEMETERY)

Makes 16 squares

Prep time: 20 minutes for the filling

Cooking time: 20 minutes (pastry)
30–35 minutes (tart)

This fruit-laden tray bake is also called Fly Cemetery because the currants and raisins look a little like dead flies! They also go by the name of Fruit Squares because they are cut into squares. They consist of a rich, dried fruit mix sandwiched between layers of pastry, and they are very moreish. I prefer raisins to currants so I put more in but you can vary the amounts of each as long as the overall quantity of dried fruit amounts to the same.

INGREDIENTS

Pastry layers

1 x quantity Sweet Shortcrust Pastry (see recipe on p. 39).

Filling

50g vegan butter

100g soft light brown sugar

250g raisins

150g currants

2 teaspoons ground mixed spice

Soya milk to glaze

Caster sugar to sprinkle

METHOD

Line a 20cm x 20cm baking tin with greaseproof baking paper.

Melt the vegan butter and sugar in a saucepan. Take off the heat and stir in the raisins, currants and mixed spice. Set aside.

Heat the oven to 180°C.

Divide your pastry into two with one piece slightly larger than the other. Roll the larger piece out on a floured surface to fit the base and sides of the baking tin and the other large enough to cover the top.

Line the baking tin with the larger piece of pastry and gently press it into the base and up the sides. Prick the base with a fork, cover with greaseproof baking paper and baking beans (or dry rice) and part-bake ('blind') for 15 minutes. Remove from the oven, take off the baking beans and baking paper and return to the oven for another 5 minutes.

Remove the tart case from the oven and spread the filling evenly over. Cover with the remaining pastry, crimping the sides with your fingers, and cut a few small slits in the top to allow steam out when baking. Brush with a little soya milk.

Bake for around 30–35 minutes or until the pastry is golden. Remove from the oven and sprinkle with a little caster sugar. Slice into squares while warm and leave to cool completely before transferring to an airtight container. These will keep for a week, if you haven't eaten them all already!

QUEEN MARY'S TART

Makes 1 x 18cm tart

Prep time: 15 minutes for the filling

Cooking time: 10–12 minutes

This tart is possibly named after Mary Queen of Scots. It also goes by the name of Edinburgh Tart and has a puff pastry base. Use a vegan-friendly shop-bought brand. Traditionally this tart contains jam, mixed dried fruit and sultanas. In this vegan version I use cherries and flaked almonds.

Tip: when using creamed coconut, the coconut and the coconut fat may separate; make sure you use some of both when measuring out your quantities.

INGREDIENTS

Tart case

Around 180g strip of vegan puff pastry (e.g. Bells)

Filling

50g vegan butter

50g soft brown sugar

100g creamed coconut

A pinch of salt

1 teaspoon vanilla extract

1 teaspoon almond extract

40g flaked almonds

40g glacé cherries, chopped finely

METHOD

Heat the oven to 220°C.

Melt the vegan butter, sugar, creamed coconut and salt together in a pan on low heat. Remove from the heat and stir in the vanilla extract, almond extract, flaked almonds and cherries.

Put the strip of pastry into an 18cm round fluted baking tin so that it covers the base and sides. Press the pastry into the fluted edges and trim away any excess and discard. Bake for 10–12 minutes and until puffed up and golden, then remove from the oven. Let sit for 5 minutes, then cut out the 'lid' of the pastry and scoop out the inside and tip the filling into the pastry case. Discard the excess pastry including the lid. Serve warm.

6

TRAY BAKES

BANANA AND SALTED DATE CARAMEL SLICES

{You can prepare the base, salted date caramel and cream a day in in advance}

Makes 8 large slices or 16 squares

Base prep time: 10 minutes

These slices are my vegan take on a banoffee pie, and are highly addictive! They comprise a date, almond, walnut and pumpkin seed base, a layer of salted date caramel, slices of banana and a layer of vegan cream.

This tray bake doesn't require baking!

INGREDIENTS

100g pitted Medjool or other soft dates

100g almonds

25g pumpkin seeds

25g shelled walnuts

A pinch of salt

1 tablespoon almond butter

You will need

1 x Base (see recipe above)

1 quantity of Salted Date Caramel (see recipe on p. 34), chilled

1 large or 2 small firm bananas, peeled and sliced thickly (to make 25 slices)

1½ quantity of Whipped Cream (see recipe on p. 40) or shop-bought vegan whipping cream, whipped and chilled

Vegan dark chocolate (at least 54% cocoa solids) to decorate

METHOD

Line a 20cm square baking tray with greaseproof baking paper.

Put all of the ingredients in a food processor bowl. Pulse 7 or 8 times and then process until the mixture has clumped together.

Tip the mixture into the tray and press the down firmly and evenly, then chill in the fridge until needed.

To Assemble the Caramel Slices

Remove the base, salted date caramel and the cream from the fridge.

Tip the salted date caramel onto the base and spread evenly. Place the slices of banana on top of the caramel layer (roughly 5 rows of 5 slices of banana). Then add the cream, smoothing it evenly over the sliced banana. Grate dark chocolate generously over the top.

Chill in the fridge until you are ready to cut into slices and serve. These will keep for 1–2 days, covered and chilled.

DATE CRUMBLE SQUARES

Makes 16 slices

Prep time: 15 minutes (date filling); 15 minutes (crumble)

Cooking time: 25–30 minutes

A real Scottish classic and found all over Scotland. I love a date crumble square with a cup of tea in the afternoon. These are the real deal: a sweet gooey date filling sandwiched between two layers of oat crumble.

INGREDIENTS

Date filling

300g pitted dates, chopped roughly

165ml cold water

1 teaspoon vanilla extract

Crumble

150g plain white flour or plain wholemeal flour

150g rolled oats

1 teaspoon baking powder

½ teaspoon bicarbonate of soda

A pinch of salt

100g demerara sugar

100g vegan butter (block butter is best, such as Naturli)

METHOD

Put the dates and water in a pan and bring them to the boil. Then reduce the heat and mash the dates into a soft pulp with the back of a spoon. Remove from the heat and set aside to cool. Once cool, stir in the vanilla extract.

While the filling is cooking, you can make the crumble mixture.

Heat the oven to 180°C. Line a 20cm x 20cm baking tin with greaseproof baking paper.

Combine the flour, oats, baking powder, bicarbonate of soda, salt and sugar in a mixing bowl. Next, cut the butter into the flour mixture and rub it in until it resembles coarse breadcrumbs. Spread half of the mixture evenly over the base of the baking tin, pressing it firmly into the base with the back of a spoon. Then spread the date filling evenly over the base. Spoon the remaining crumble mixture into the tin and press it firmly into the date filling.

Bake for 25–30 minutes until golden brown. Remove from the oven and cool completely before cutting into squares. These will keep in an airtight container for 2–3 days.

FLAPJACKS

Makes 16 squares

Prep time: 10 minutes

Cooking time: 15–18 minutes

The basic Scottish flapjack recipe contains butter, golden syrup and oats. This vegan deluxe version adds hazelnuts, pumpkin seeds, sesame seeds and dried cranberries. You can substitute the nuts, seeds and dried fruit with your favourites; just keep the weight ratios the same as in the recipe.

INGREDIENTS

150g vegan butter

180g golden syrup

200g porridge oats

50g hazelnuts, chopped roughly

50g pumpkin seeds

30g sesame seeds

30g dried cranberries (or dried cherries)

METHOD

Heat the oven to 180°C. Line a 20cm square baking tin with greaseproof baking paper.

Melt the butter and golden syrup together in a large pan. Remove from the heat and stir in the oats, hazelnuts, pumpkin seeds, sesame seeds and dried cranberries (or dried cherries if using) until well combined.

Tip the mixture into the baking tin and spread evenly. Bake in the oven for about 15–18 minutes or until golden brown. Remove from the oven and cool completely before cutting into squares. These will keep for around 5 days in an airtight container.

A word about . . . seeds

Pumpkin seeds are a good source of antioxidants and heart-healthy fats. They also contain protein, fibre, magnesium, potassium, zinc and iron. Add them to breakfast cereals and muesli and porridge as well as to muffins, cakes and biscuits. Sesame seeds are also a good source of antioxidants and contain protein as well as healthy fats and fibre. They are also a source of calcium, iron, potassium, magnesium, B-vitamins and vitamin E. Add them to savoury biscuits such as oatcakes and to bread mixes.

GINGER, RAISIN AND NUT TIFFIN

Makes 12 slices

Prep time: 20 minutes

Said to originate in Troon on the west coast of Scotland in the early 1900s, this tray bake traditionally consisted of crushed biscuits, butter, sugar and raisins. I have jazzed it up by adding golden syrup, dark chocolate, stem ginger and pecan nuts. While this is a sweet treat, it is worth noting that pecan nuts contain antioxidants as well as vitamins and minerals such as manganese, potassium, calcium, iron, magnesium, zinc and selenium.

INGREDIENTS

100g vegan butter

50g soft brown sugar

50g golden syrup

A pinch of salt

140g vegan dark chocolate (70% cocoa solids), chopped roughly

1 teaspoon ground ginger

100g raisins

2 pieces stem ginger in syrup, chopped finely

80g hazelnuts or pecans, chopped roughly

250g vegan digestive biscuits (shop-bought or see recipe for Digestive Biscuits on p. 46), crushed

METHOD

Line a 20cm square baking tin with greaseproof baking paper.

Put the vegan butter, sugar, golden syrup, salt and dark chocolate in a bowl over a saucepan of simmering water ensuring the pan doesn't touch the water and stir until melted. Remove from the heat and stir in the ground ginger followed by the raisins, stem ginger, nuts and crushed digestive biscuits and mix together well.

Tip the mixture into the tin and smooth the surface with the back of a spoon or palette knife.

Refrigerate for at least two hours before cutting into 12 pieces. Remove from the baking tin and wrap in kitchen foil and store in the fridge. The tiffin will keep for at least a week.

MILLIONAIRE'S SHORTBREAD

Makes 16

Shortbread Base prep time: 15 minutes

Cooking time: 35–40 minutes

Also known as caramel shortbread, these are probably the most decadent of the shortbreads and a treat for an afternoon tea party. Millionaire's Shortbread is rich, gooey, crunchy and chocolatey and comprises a layer of shortbread, a layer of caramel and a layer of chocolate: triple delight!

INGREDIENTS

150g soft vegan butter (such as Vitalite)

75g caster sugar

225g plain white flour

Caramel

Makes 1 quantity

Prep time: 10–15 minutes + cooling time

175g soft vegan butter (such as Vitalite)

140g light brown sugar

50ml golden syrup

50ml full-fat coconut milk

¼ teaspoon sea salt

1 teaspoon vanilla extract

Chocolate topping

Makes 200g

Prep time: 10 minutes + chilling time

200g vegan dark chocolate (at least 56% cocoa solids) broken into pieces

1 tablespoon coconut butter

A pinch of sea salt

METHOD

Heat the oven to 180°C. Line a 20cm square baking tin with greaseproof baking paper.

Cream the vegan butter and sugar together in a bowl. Stir in the flour and bring the mixture together with a fork and then with your hands to form a soft dough. Press the dough evenly into the base of the baking tin and prick it all over with a fork. Bake in the oven for 35–40 minutes or until golden on top. Remove from the oven and cool in the tin and then in the fridge before making the caramel.

Caramel

Heat all of the ingredients in a heavy-based pan on low to medium heat, stirring until the sugar has dissolved. Bring to the boil then keep on a rolling boil for around 10 minutes, stirring continuously, until the caramel has thickened. Remove from the heat and pour over the chilled shortbread base. Leave to cool for 30 minutes then refrigerate for at least two hours. Then make the chocolate topping.

Chocolate Topping

Add the chocolate to a *bain marie* or heatproof bowl over a saucepan of simmering water making sure the bowl doesn't touch the water and melt it. Once the chocolate has melted stir in the coconut butter and the salt. Remove from the heat, tip the chocolate over the set caramel and smooth the top with a palette knife. Cool in the fridge for at least 30 minutes or until the chocolate has set. Remove from the fridge and allow the shortbread to come to room temperature then cut into 16 squares using a hot sharp knife. The shortbread will keep for several days stored in the fridge if it is not eaten at first sitting!

ON-THE-GO OAT BARS

Makes 12 bars

Prep time: 15 minutes

Cooking time: 12–15 minutes

These oat bars are full of healthy nuts, seeds and dried fruit and are packed with energy. They are also an ideal way to introduce blackstrap molasses (which contains some calcium) into your baking. Ideal for kiddies' lunch boxes or a post-exercise snack. These can be cut into rectangular bars, squares or smaller bite-sized pieces.

If you like a softer, chewier bar, add 1 tablespoon of plain flour to the oat mixture.

INGREDIENTS

200g porridge oats

1 tablespoon ground flax seeds

30g hazelnuts, chopped roughly

30g walnuts, chopped roughly

30g almonds, chopped roughly

30g sesame seeds

30g pumpkin seeds

6 dried apricots, chopped roughly

3 pitted Medjool dates or other soft dates, chopped roughly

A pinch of salt

90g smooth almond butter or peanut butter

3 tablespoons blackstrap molasses or black treacle

3 tablespoons maple syrup

1 teaspoon vanilla extract

METHOD

Heat the oven to 180°C.

Line a 20cm square baking tin with greaseproof baking paper.

Mix the oats, flax seeds, hazelnuts, walnuts, almonds, sesame seeds, pumpkin seeds, apricots, dates and salt in a bowl.

Melt the almond butter or peanut butter, blackstrap molasses or black treacle and maple syrup in a saucepan on low heat. Remove from the heat and stir in the vanilla essence. Add the wet ingredients to the dry ingredients and mix thoroughly.

Tip the mixture into baking tin and press it firmly into the base, then bake in the oven for 12–15 minutes.

Remove from the oven and cool completely in the tin before cutting. These will keep for at least a week in an airtight container.

Variations

Use the same quantity of Brazil nuts, pecans and pistachios (also chopped roughly), in place of the other nuts.

Use raisins or sultanas, goji berries, dried blueberries or dried sour cherries instead of the dates or apricots.

PEAR, COCONUT AND WALNUT FLAPJACKS

Makes 16 squares

Prep time: 20 minutes

Cooking time: 18–20 minutes

A variation on a traditional flapjack, these are free from refined sugar and fat and include dried fruit, nut butter and walnuts for a healthier, energy-providing snack bar. Substitute the standard porridge oats with gluten-free oats for a gluten-free treat.

INGREDIENTS

125g smooth almond butter or peanut butter

125ml date syrup or maple syrup

200g porridge oats

1 teaspoon ground ginger

A pinch of salt

50g dried pears, chopped roughly

50g desiccated coconut

40g walnuts, chopped roughly

METHOD

Heat the oven to 180°C and line a 20cm square baking tin with greaseproof baking paper.

Melt the nut butter and syrup in a large pan. Remove from the heat and stir in the oats, ginger, salt, pears, coconut and walnuts until well combined.

Tip the mixture into the base of the baking tin and spread evenly. Bake for 18–20 minutes. Remove from the oven and cool in the tin before cutting into squares. These will keep for around a week in an airtight container.

TRIPLE CHOCOLATE BROWNIES

Makes 16

Prep time: 20 minutes

Cooking time: 20–25 minutes

Although not strictly Scottish, brownies are so ubiquitous in Scottish cafés and such a popular home-cooked tray bake, that they make it into the book. These brownies come out more 'gooey' rather than 'cakey' in the great debate about brownie consistency. Serve with raspberries and a dusting of icing sugar or with vegan whipped cream for a really indulgent treat.

INGREDIENTS

2 tablespoons ground flax seeds

6 tablespoons cold water

120g vegan dark chocolate (at least 56% cocoa solids)

150g plain flour

1 teaspoon baking powder

3 rounded tablespoons cacao powder or cocoa powder

100g dark muscovado or dark brown sugar

½ teaspoon sea salt flakes

45ml olive or rapeseed oil

50ml hot water

30g vegan chocolate chips or chunks

METHOD

Heat the oven to 180°C. Line a 20cm square baking tin with greaseproof baking parchment.

Mix together the flax seeds and water in a cup and set aside to gel and form flax eggs.

Melt the chocolate in a *bain marie* or heatproof bowl over a saucepan of simmering water, making sure the bowl doesn't touch the water. Set aside to cool a little.

Mix together the flour, baking powder, cacao or cocoa powder, sugar and salt in a bowl.

Add the oil, flax eggs, melted chocolate and hot water and stir until well combined. The mixture will be quite thick. Tip into the prepared baking tin, sprinkle over the chocolate chips and bake for 20–25 minutes. Remove from the oven and cool completely in the tin before cutting into squares. The brownies will keep 2–3 days in an airtight container.

7

THE COOKIE SHINE
(SCOTTISH AFTERNOON TEA)

CARROT LOX (VEGAN SMOKED SALMON)

{Prepare in advance}

Makes 1 x 350ml jar

Prep time: 15 minutes

Cooking time: 8–10 minutes

A NOTE ON THE COOKIE SHINE

A cookie shine is an old Scottish term for afternoon tea. While I have suggested a selection of savoury and sweet recipes in this section which might grace your cake stand, and which I think combine well together, of course your cookie shine can consist of any range of sandwiches, scones, biscuits, cakes and other treats.

CARROT LOX (VEGAN SMOKED SALMON)

This recipe is effectively for pickled carrots! I first tasted vegan smoked salmon in a vegan café in Edinburgh and have reconstructed the recipe here. It is a lovely fresh dish. I serve it with the Seed Crackers (see recipe on p. 84) although you will love it with vegan cream cheese on bagels too.

INGREDIENTS

40ml apple cider vinegar or rice vinegar

200ml hot water

2 teaspoons soy sauce

1 teaspoon black treacle

½ teaspoon smoked paprika

2 medium carrots, peeled into ribbons

2 teaspoons chopped fresh dill

METHOD

Place the vinegar, water, soy sauce, treacle and smoked paprika in a saucepan. Bring to the boil, then add the carrot ribbons, reduce the heat to a simmer and cook for around 8–10 minutes or until the carrots have softened.

Ladle the mixture into a lidded jar then stir in the dill. Leave to cool completely then seal and refrigerate overnight.

When you are ready to serve the lox, remove what you need and drain it from the brine.

MUSHROOM VOL-AU-VENTS

{Prepare in advance}

Makes 10 vol-au-vents

Prep time: 10 minutes

Cooking time: 20 minutes

These puff pastry delights are a little bit retro! They remind me of the 1970s, when a mushroom vol-au-vent was a buffet party highlight. Luckily, they never go out of fashion, and are perfect for afternoon tea as part of your savoury platter.

Mushroom filling

Makes enough mixture to fill 10 small vol-au-vents

Prep time: 10 minutes

Cooking time: 5 minutes

INGREDIENTS

Vol-Au-Vent cases

200g vegan puff pastry (e.g. Bells)

Plain white flour for dusting

Soya milk to glaze

Mushroom filling

250g chestnut or button mushrooms, chopped finely

1 tablespoon vegan butter

1 garlic clove, crushed or chopped finely

½ teaspoon dried oregano

150ml soya cream or oat cream

1 teaspoon cornflour mixed with a little soya milk

½ teaspoon English mustard

Salt and black pepper

METHOD

Line a baking tray with greaseproof baking paper. Heat the oven to 190°C.

Roll out the puff pastry on a floured surface until around 5–6mm thick. Cut out the vol-au-vents with a 6–7cm biscuit cutter. Using a smaller biscuit cutter of around 4–5cm make an impression on each vol-au-vent case but do not cut all the way through.

Place on the baking tray, brush with a little soya milk and bake for around 20 minutes until puffed up and golden. Transfer to a wire rack to cool completely.

Once cool, cut out the smaller circles and set these aside as your 'hats'. Scoop out the pastry inside and discard, leaving the shell for your filling. Fill with the Mushroom Filling (see recipe below) and place the 'hats' on top. Cool and keep in the fridge until ready to serve. Serve at room temperature. These are best eaten the day they are made. You can also serve them hot or warm if you prefer, in which case prepare your filling while the vol-au-vent cases are cooking.

Mushroom Filling

Cook the mushrooms in the vegan butter on medium heat until softened and most of the liquid from the mushrooms has evaporated. Then add the garlic and oregano and cook for a minute. Add the cream and the cornflour mixture and cook until the cream has thickened. Stir in the mustard and season to taste with salt and pepper.

NAE EGG AND WATERCRESS SANDWICHES

Nae Egg filling

Makes enough mixture to fill 3–4 sandwiches

Preparation time: 15 minutes

This sandwich filling can be turned into a canapé on a buffet or a bite-size savoury choice for afternoon tea. The recipe uses tofu to replace the egg which also has the benefit of adding calcium to the dish. To achieve a flavour akin to 'egginess', you can use kala namak (black salt) although use ordinary salt if you prefer.

INGREDIENTS

1 x 300g block of silken tofu, drained

2 tablespoons vegan mayonnaise

½ teaspoon English mustard

A squeeze of lemon juice

A large pinch of salt or kala namak (black salt) (optional)

3–4 twists of pepper

Two spring onions, chopped finely

A large pinch of turmeric

To serve: wholemeal or granary bread (see recipe on p.80 or use your favourite loaf); watercress (or salad leaves)

METHOD

In a medium bowl, place all of the ingredients in the order they are given above and then mash with a fork to resemble egg mayonnaise. Add further lemon juice or (black) salt to taste or turmeric for colour.

To serve, cut slices of wholemeal or granary bread and spread generous amounts of the filling onto your bottom slices of bread. Then add the watercress or lettuce leaves and top with another slice of bread. Cut each sandwich into four triangles.

TOONA SANDWICHES

Makes enough mixture to fill 3–4 sandwiches

Prep time: 15 minutes

This is my vegan version of 'tuna', made with chickpeas, which gets its taste of the sea from the addition of capers. While 'toona' is ideal as a sandwich filling, it is also a tasty topping on oatcakes and crackers or on a baked potato.

INGREDIENTS

1 x 400g tin of chickpeas, drained and rinsed

3 tablespoons vegan mayonnaise

2 teaspoons lemon juice

½ teaspoon English mustard

2 teaspoons capers, drained and chopped finely

1 celery stalk, trimmed and chopped finely

8–10 chives chopped finely to make 1 heaped tablespoon (or 1 spring onion, chopped finely)

Black pepper

Sea salt

To serve: wholemeal or granary bread; watercress (or salad leaves)

METHOD

Place the chickpeas, mayonnaise, lemon juice, mustard and capers in a bowl and mash with a fork or potato masher until well mashed. Next, add the celery and chives (or spring onions) and mash again until you reach the consistency you prefer (either smooth or with some chunks of chickpea remaining). Season to taste with black pepper and salt (if needed – the capers are salty as they are stored in brine). Then chill in the fridge until needed.

To serve, cut slices of wholemeal or granary bread and spread with the 'Toona' mixture. Then add watercress or lettuce leaves. Top with further slices of bread and cut each sandwich into four triangles.

BEETROOT AND HAZELNUT TRUFFLES

{Prepare in advance}

Makes around 12 small or 6–8 large truffles

Prep time: 15 minutes

This no-bake treat is free from refined sugar and full of goodness garnered from the beetroot, dates, cacao, almond butter and hazelnuts. It adds a little twist to an afternoon tea party and shows that raw sweets can be delicious. You can also roll the truffles in cacao nibs or desiccated coconut instead of chopped hazelnuts as an alternative.

INGREDIENTS

1 small cooked beetroot (not in vinegar), about 30g, chopped roughly

8 pitted Medjool dates, chopped roughly

1 teaspoon vanilla extract

2 rounded tablespoons cacao powder or cocoa powder

2 tablespoons smooth almond butter (or smooth unsweetened peanut butter)

A pinch of salt

35g roasted chopped hazelnuts + extra if needed

METHOD

Place all of the ingredients, except the chopped hazelnuts, in the nut grinder of a food processor and pulse until a sticky dough forms.

Tip the ground hazelnuts onto a plate. Take a spoonful of the truffle mixture and with your hands roll it into a ball, then roll it in the chopped hazelnuts ensuring that the entire surface is coated. Repeat until all of the mixture has been used up. Transfer the truffles to a clean plate, cover and chill. Remove from the fridge about 30 minutes before you want to serve them. They will keep for up to a week in the fridge.

FLORENTINES WITH APRICOTS AND STEM GINGER

Makes about 16 small florentines

Prep time: 15 minutes

Cooking time: 10–12 minutes

These are the perfect chocolate-coated, bite-sized luxury and also make lovely edible gifts. Dried apricots contain beneficial nutrients including beta carotene, vitamin E, calcium, potassium, vitamin C and fibre, while the stem ginger provides a gentle heat to this sweet treat.

INGREDIENTS

30g vegan butter

40g demerara sugar

1 tablespoon golden syrup

2 teaspoons oat cream or soya cream (optional)

A pinch of salt

40g dried apricots, chopped finely

2 pieces stem ginger in syrup, chopped finely (about 30g)

40g candied mixed peel

60g blanched flaked almonds

25g brazil nuts, chopped finely

10g plain white flour

100g vegan dark chocolate (at least 56% cocoa solids), broken into pieces

METHOD

Heat the oven to 180°C. Line two baking trays with greaseproof baking paper.

Melt the butter, sugar and golden syrup together in a large pan until the sugar has dissolved. Remove from the heat and stir in the cream, if using, and salt.

Put the apricots, stem ginger, mixed peel, flaked almonds and brazil nuts in a bowl, then mix in the flour. Then add the fruit mixture to the melted butter mixture and stir until well combined. Place teaspoons of the mixture onto the baking trays and flatten them out leaving space between each florentine as they will spread while baking. You can also use a biscuit cutter to shape the mixture.

Bake for around 10–12 minutes, leave to cool for 2–3 minutes on the baking trays then transfer (a spatula is useful here) to a wire rack to cool completely.

Once cool, melt the chocolate in a *bain marie* or a heatproof bowl placed over a pan of simmering water, making sure the bowl doesn't touch the water.

Turn the florentines over and cover with chocolate. Then make a wavy pattern through the chocolate with a fork. Leave to cool completely. These will keep for up to a week in an airtight container.

LEMON CURD TARTS

{Prepare in advance}

Makes 6

Prep time: 15 minutes

These little delicacies are ideal for an afternoon tea cake stand and combine a zingy lemony filling with a sweet date and nut tart case. They are delightful to eat. You could also make one large tart if you prefer.

INGREDIENTS

Base

1 x recipe for Sweet Date and Nut Tart Case (see p. 38)

Filling

1 x recipe for Lemon Curd (see p. 31)

METHOD

Place 6 paper cupcake cases in 6 of the holes of a 12-hole muffin tin. Using a dessert spoon, scoop some of the date and nut mixture into each cupcake case and press it firmly into the base and sides using the back of a spoon to mould a hollow in the middle. Refrigerate for at least 30 minutes.

Remove from the fridge and carefully remove the paper from around the date and nut tart cases. Then fill each tart with the lemon curd. Refrigerate until needed. Best eaten the day they are made.

STRAWBERRY SHORTBREAD ROUNDS

Makes around 20 biscuits

Prep time: 15 minutes

Cooking time: 15–20 minutes

This recipe uses the classic 3:2:1 ratio of flour to butter and sugar to make dainty shortbread rounds topped with cream and a strawberry which make a lovely afternoon tea treat. They are a little bit scrumptious!

INGREDIENTS

100g soft vegan butter (such as Vitalite)

50g caster sugar + extra for sprinkling

150g plain white flour

Topping

Whipped Cream (see recipe on p. 40)

About 20 strawberries

Icing sugar (optional)

METHOD

Heat the oven to 180°C. Line a baking tray with greaseproof baking paper.

Cream the vegan butter and sugar together in a bowl. Stir in the flour and bring the mixture together with your hands to form a soft dough. Roll out the dough on a lightly dusted worktop until around 1cm thick. Then cut out small circles with a biscuit cutter. Transfer the shortbread onto the baking tray, then lightly prick the surface of each shape with a fork. Bake in the oven for 15–20 minutes or until the shortbread is golden in colour. Remove from the oven for 5 minutes then transfer to a wire rack to cool completely. These will keep in an airtight container for 2–3 days.

When you are ready to serve, add a dollop of whipped cream to each biscuit, followed by a whole strawberry. Dust with a little icing sugar if liked. Best eaten within a few hours of making as the cream will soften the shortbread.

FURTHER READING

Scottish Baking

My Wee Granny's Bannocks and Bakes by Angela Hossack, Independent, 2018
New Scottish Baking by Sue Lawrence, Birlinn Ltd, 2024
The Glasgow Cookery Book: Celebrating 100 Years of the Dough School by Glasgow Queen's College, Waverley Books Ltd, 2009
The Scottish Baking Bible by Liz Ashworth, Birlinn Ltd, 2020

Vegan Baking

Simply Vegan Baking by Freya Cox, Murdoch Books, 2022
The Little Book of Vegan Bakes by Holly Jade, Ebury Press, 2022
The Vegan Baker by Dunja Gulin, Ryland Peters & Small, 2017
Vegan Baking for Beginners by J L Fields, Rockridge Press, 2020

ACKNOWLEDGEMENTS

A cookery book doesn't get made by one person and I have a debt of thanks to many people who have helped along the way: to the former tutors and fellow tutees at Demuths Cookery School, as was, in Bath and Melusine in the South of France (https://www.melusinefrance.com/), especially Rachel Demuth and Helen Lawrence.

A million thanks to all the brilliant team at Birlinn especially to Andrew, El and Debs. And to Mark Blackadder, and to Zoe Ross for compiling the index.

Heartfelt thanks to Heather Porteous for friendship and being my chief taster, to Carolyn Barr, Frankie Barr, Senga Bate, Kate Chedgzoy, Cathy Clay, Jude Crichton, Bill Crook, David Johnson, Craig Jones, Heather Jones, Gerri Kimber, Michael Law, Neil McGillivray, Ian Miller, Rosanne Murphy, Gill Plain, Dominique Seetim, Olga Taxidou and Andrew Torrance for food conversations, baking ingredients, testing and tasting, love, friendship and support.

A shout out to John Glynn for taking me back to photography via the Botanics.

Most of all my special thanks to Sandy Paterson, for believing in me.

This book is dedicated to my dad, Clifford Brian Jones (1935–2023), who loved fruitcake and fruity buns.

INDEX

First published in 2024 by
Birlinn Limited
West Newington House
10 Newington Road
Edinburgh EH9 1QS

www.birlinn.co.uk

ISBN 978 178027 872 8

British Library Cataloguing in Publication Data
A catalogue record for this book is available from the British Library.

Designed and typeset by Mark Blackadder

Printed and bound by PNB Print, Latvia